"This book is very informative and covers everything I could think of, as well as being enjoyable and entertaining to read."
-- Gary Wallut, Retired
Missouri Department of Natural Resources Park Ranger and
Resource Manager for Harry S. Truman State Park

"Camping in a Pop-Up Camper is Paradise is a personal and enthusiastic guide filled with information that can make what could be a camping disaster into a total learning experience before-hand without the pit-falls of failure. Mellody's wholesome approach toward the 'camper's code' is just what every park attendant and/or custodian would like to say to every camper (new or old) given the opportunity. However, simply put - just remember G.R.E.E.N.!"
-- Doyel Roller,
50-Year Camping Enthusiast and U.S. Army
Corps of Engineers Camp Ground Park Attendant

"Mellody successfully educates and assists those interested in camping and enjoyment of the outdoors in a fun and safe manner. The first aid included in this book includes a good representation of approaches to a variety of medical situations and problems which may be encountered with such activities."
-- Linda M. Wilson, D.O.
American Osteopathic Association Member and
American College of Osteopathic Family Physicians Member

"This how-to book is a camping encyclopedia in condensed form. While comprehensive, it is an easy read as Mellody tells humorous tales of her own beginning mistakes. Her tips on conservation are right on the money and, if followed, will ensure our waterways stay clean for generations to come."
-- Kathryn Lackman,
Missouri Department of Conservation Stream Team Volunteer
Water Quality Monitoring Research Assistant

Camping in a Pop-Up Camper is Paradise

A carry-along guide for novice & experienced camping enthusiasts interested in tent-trailer camping.

by
Mellody R. L. Allee

Camping in a Pop-Up Camper is Paradise

A carry-along guide for novice & experienced camping enthusiasts interested in tent-trailer camping.

ISBN: 978-160844-540-0
First published by Dog Ear Publishing

Acknowledgements

Thank you to each and every person who read my book and gave me helpful suggestions. It is much better than it would have been without your constructive critiques.

In my attempt to string words together that were neither too technical nor too boring, Gary Wallut was key. Doyel Roller reminded me of all the issues our campsite custodians encounter that we tend to take for granted - until they are not up to standard. Kathryn Lackman helped me report on caring for our waterways and lakes.

Linda Wilson made sure I wrote the right amount of first aid and that the first aid I wrote was correct. My favorite daughter-in-law, Lori Allee, suggested several (many) word changes that led to sentence improvement.

CW4 Don Case, Ret., did his best to keep me out of the weeds and on the pop-up camping track. For one thing, he made sure that all of my military acronymns were defined. Best of all, he had no fear of hurting my feelings by correcting anything! He knew I would "soldier up."

Millie Little, my mom, was a little more hesitant to make suggestions that might hurt my feelings, but in the end, she also came through for me.

My professors at Missouri Valley College in Marshall, MO, were the best a person could ask for! Loren Gruber never doubted I would be published one day. Sister Kathryn Wildt challenged me to think higher and deeper. Dale and Virginia Zank have never quit asking when my novel would be finished. Their belief in me is humbling. I know they will be tickled to see this book published and I promise, guys, I really will get the novel finished! Promise!

My best friend and hero - my husband, Steve - tells me all my ideas are great and then he helps me accomplish all of my goals. There are not enough words in the English language to tell him how much he is appreciated and loved.

Last, but by no means least, I give my thanks to Jesus Christ, my Lord and Savior, for all the many blessings He has given me.

Meal Chapters, Courses and Contents

~ A Young Whitetail Doe ~
It is her home, we are just visitors.
Please help keep her home G.R.E.E.N.

Foreword

This is a very light, great reading book on the art and science of just plain having fun camping. I think this is a must read for the novice or beginner who has always wanted to visit the great outdoors but was reluctant to do so.

I worked for 30 years for the United States Forest Service and have witnessed many things during my career. Most memorable were those individuals who ventured into the back country unprepared. It was most evident those unprepared would ultimately have to be rescued. If they had taken the time to gain some knowledge about leaving a home environment for an event into the forests and back country, they would have saved themselves a good deal of trauma.

Mellody has captured some great insights that perhaps will assist some with having a good time rather than having a negative experience. Based on her numerous trips into the field, she has captured a great check list of do's and don'ts for those who are contemplating their first trip or those who are returning from their first experience and want to continue.

I highly recommend this book; it is informative, full of humor and written with lots of personal funny stories.

~ *Dr. Donald M. Case, PhD*
US Forest Service, Retired

Preface

My goal when starting this book was to create a guide for the average family of pop-up tent trailer campers. Most of us are not retired and I would guess that few of us are independently wealthy. At least not the people I know. We may camp economically, but we refuse to give up our luxuries!

With the cost of gasoline spiraling into the ozone, my scope suddenly got larger. Many motor home RVers and full-size hard-side caravan camper owners are "downsizing" to pop-ups. They are easier to pull than a hard-sided caravan or fifth-wheel camper and are more economical when it comes to gasoline usage than either a motor home RV or a camping trailer. For the RVer who is "downsizing," this book may give you some insight that will help make your pop-up experience as enjoyable, if not more so, than your RV experience.

While some may think they are trading "down" when they purchase their new or newly used pop-up camper, in the eyes of devotees to pop-ups, we know they are really trading "up." A pop-up provides most of the comforts of an RV or a caravan, as well as letting the beauty of nature surround you, just like tent camping.

However, the pop-up, especially one equipped with an air conditioner and furnace, also provides for more protection from Mother Nature when she is, well, showing her nature, so to speak. You know what I mean! I am talking about those trips when it is either 120 degrees Fahrenheit or it rains for the entire trip. For getting back to nature without Mother Nature ruining your trip, pop-up campers are the ultimate in camping!

I am not a mechanic. I am not an engineer. I do not know how all of the axles and cables work on my pop-up; I just know how to make them operate. So this guide is not filled with a lot of technical specs about tent campers. There is a short chapter on basic maintenance to make your camper last longer, but that is about as technical as I get.

And, in all honesty, I picked my husband's brain to complete that chapter since he, himself, could write the definitive book on the mechanics of it all.

This guide is filled with information on how to make your camping experience enjoyable. Hopefully, it will help you make some good memories and start a few new traditions. That way, when you are sitting in your living room in the deep of winter, you can relax and remember your awesome summer camping trips. (Because with the convenience of a pop-up, you can take more than just one!)

I hope everyone who reads this book will either pick up an idea or at least have a good laugh at some of the mistakes my husband and I have made along the way. Do not worry about making mistakes, go camping and make sure you do it your way. Half the fun of the trip is seeing just how relaxing you can make your camping trip. With a little preparation and know-how, almost everyone can enjoy camping. Even if you are starting out in a tent and not a pop-up, this is a book you can use. Do give camping a try. Camping is one of the few vacation experiences that can be as economical or as extravagant as your pocket book can afford. It can be as close to the back door as you want to stay or as far away in the back forty as you have time to drive.

When you finally get a campfire going and the marshmallows roasted, there is nothing quite like sitting in the dark and having a quiet conversation. If you are lucky, there will be no campers nearby who have music blaring, no dogs will be incessantly barking, and you will be able to listen to the sounds of nature; the birds chirping in the tree tops, or the lake water lapping at the shore.

Quite truthfully, with our busy lifestyles of today, there really is not a better way to let the peace and quiet of the universe seep into your soul as camping. I encourage everyone to give it a try. It truly is a special experience.

Mellody R. L. Allee

Tent Camping, 1991

First Camper, 1992: Look how bare our
campsite is - but we had our bikes!

Chapter One
~ The Appetizer ~
Beginning the Experience

Getting Ready to Have Fun!

In case you are wondering about the author of this book, let me introduce myself. My camping experience began in tents and not a pop-up; so, I believe a confession is in order. Before I had my first camping trip, I did not have a book. I could not read any instructions or any introduction. I could not even look at pictures in a book. I did, however, have about six drill sergeants screaming in my ear telling me what to pack. My guess was, *they* probably had written a book. I did not question them one tiny bit! To be totally honest, I avoided eye contact at all costs! (Eye contact usually meant one would end up in the front leaning rest position. Hah. There is no rest to it. You are doing pushups! Lots and lots of pushups.)

On some of those military camping trips, I carried everything I needed to survive on my back in my rucksack. This does teach one how to pack efficiently, but I kind of like to actually enjoy my civilian camping trips and I want them to be a little more enjoyable than enduring at the survivor level.

I want electricity! I want make-up! I want a hot shower more than every third day! I want a blow dryer and a curling iron! I want a roof over my head and a bed to sleep in. In other words, I want comfort with a capital C! Actually, on second thought, make that a capital C.O.M.F.O.R.T!

Having confessed that I want comfort does not mean I always had comfort. I have camped at one time or another in pup tents, regular tents, camping trailers, cabins, and pop-up tent campers, I believe the latter is the ultimate way to camp. For the past thirty years, I have camped weekends in a pup tent, I have camped for weeks at a time in a camping trailer, and I have camped for months at a time in a GP medium (Army lingo for a general purpose medium-sized tent). With all this camping, the most enjoyable times I have had have been in a pop-up tent camper.

You may also be wondering why the chapters are titled as food courses. The answer is another insight to my personality. I do two things *really, really well* when I am camping. First of all, I can take relaxing to new levels of contented ecstasy. Secondly, when camping, my husband and I eat like royalty. No, I do not mean filet mignon and lobster. I mean exceptional flavor with a minimum of effort in a setting no restaurant could begin to emulate. (Emeril, eat your heart out!)

I do a third thing moderately well when camping. I take pictures. A lot of pictures. I take pictures of nature and I take pictures of animals with a long zoom lens. Throughout the book I hope you enjoy scenes of some of our trips.

Now you know a little about why I love camping in general, let me expand on why I love pop-up camping in particular. All camping trips are different. With a tent camping trip, you have to pack literally everything you want to take with you virtually every time you want to go camping. There is nothing wrong with this method of camping. It is how my husband and I started out camping and we had fun every time we went somewhere. But, tent camping is labor intensive in many ways and definitely for the young in body.

After packing the tent, the bed, the bedding, the light, a small propane canister, clothes, hygiene items, food, dishes, soap, towels, a dish rag, glasses, pots and pans (which I soon learned to use as my dishwashing pans also), I was too tired to go camping! Not really. But, I did quickly figure out that anything - and I mean anything - that could be used in more than one way was, and is, a definite item to consider when packing for tent camping.

However, all the packing, unpacking, loading, and

unloading aside, one of the biggest drawbacks to tent camping (to me anyway), is the fact that the only thing we ever did in the tent was sleep, dress, and undress. Everything else that we did camping we did out in the open around the campfire.

For the family who is tent camping, on most nights this will be okay. Unfortunately, there are times when the mosquitoes will just about carry you off. If you happen to be camping in a State or National Park, in most of them you cannot use any type of mosquito lamp, yard bug spray, or bug zapper to kill them. The best you can hope for is a citronella candle or a lot of smoke from your campfire to help keep them at bay.

Then, there are other tent camping trips when it rains continuously and the wind blows so hard that your tents will literally be blown away. This has happened to my husband and I. And, if you knew my husband, and how very detail oriented he can be, you would know just how hard the wind was blowing for that feat to be accomplished! When he battens down the hatches, he battens them down.

The back of our 2002 home on wheels.
(We are still bike riding.)

That means our tents were staked, our canvases were tied, and everything should have been hunky dory. It was not. We got blown away. The campsite had a gale-force wind blow through it one night and our tent did not stand a chance.

Read the Instructions

One particular military tent camping experience stands out in my mind. There were four of us female soldiers in a GP Small. (Army lingo for a "general purpose small tent.") We were in a very cold state of our great Union and we were conducting winter training. There was snow on the ground ten inches deep, but we felt snug and warm inside our tent with our nice hot stove.

Unfortunately, no matter how hard we had tried when we were setting up our tent, we could not get the center pole to extend up all the way. At one point we got the pole up so far that it seemed to get stuck and we could not get it back down either. We felt that we would be safe putting it into the center of the tent and going ahead and using it. Ha! That was wishful thinking gone amuck.

There we were sleeping soundly - two officers and two NCOs - one a senior noncom - (acronym and abbreviation for Noncommissioned Officer - the backbone of the Army). At about 2:00 in the morning the center pole started collapsing, whether from gravity or the wind buffeting the pole, who knows? All we four female soldiers knew was the tent was coming down and we had a hot stove in the middle of it. Hot stove. Flammable canvas. Hmmmh. That scenario tends to make a person move fast!

Imagine, if you will, four half-asleep, bleary-eyed female soldiers jumping out of their sleeping bags in various styles of night dress and PJ's, yanking on combat boots - forget socks and lacing the boots - we were running outside to pull the tent lines tight so we would not have to pay the Army for a tent we burned down! Which was the exact wrong thing to do. Why? Because then when we went back inside to extend the center pole again, we had the outside lines so tight there was no way in Hades that pole was extending to any height at all. So there we were running back outside, PJ's flapping in the cold and icy wind, to loosen the ropes before we ran back inside once again to extend the pole. The cursed pole finally did extend to its full height and lock in place correctly.

All I can say is thank God there were no male soldiers awake to witness our debacle. We would have never lived it down. That qualifies, I think, as my worst tent camping experience, although I am happy to be able to laugh at it now!

The Bottom Line:

Which, finally, brings me to the point I am trying to make. If you have the chance, set your pop-up camper up in your back yard before you plan on using it for the first time.

Trust me, campers are a voyeuristic lot, and we watch every camper that moves into the campground. We sneak peeks out of the corners of our eyes so we will know who our neighbors are - for security purposes, of course. We casually stroll by to get some water from the water hydrant - or to see if we can help them set up. And, we ride our bikes for exercise around the campground, so naturally we see you set up then.

Yeah, right. We are not checking out new neighbors for security purposes. We are probably not going to help you set up - we have already had that pleasure with our own camper. We already have our water, and, the bikes are for fun and convenience. Who wants to exercise when camping for fun?

What we are really doing, is watching new campers move into place so we can check out any nifty-difty new camping gadget the neighbor might have. If they provide entertainment while setting up, all the better. Give it time. You will become voyeuristic also. It is ingrained in campers.

Popping Up Your Pop-Up

A "Baker's Dozen" Steps

Step One ~ Removing Accessories: If you have a luggage rack or bike rack on top of your camper, remove any luggage or bikes on or in them now! It might be just a wee bit hard to remove them when your roof is ten feet up in the air! (Okay, I might have learned by mistake here... Quit laughing. It is not easy to get a bike off of a pop-up roof when it is already in the air. Alright, go ahead and laugh. I did.)

Step Two ~ Expansion: Make sure you leave enough room on all sides of the camper to pull out your beds and/or slideout, and to perhaps set up an awning, when you have your pop-up totally opened. This includes making sure you have enough room overhead to actually raise your pop-up camper. Tree limbs in campsites can be low.

Step Three ~ Leveling: Now that you have ensured you have enough room for expansion, you need to make sure your pop-up is level before you open it up. Most campsites, whether gravel or grass, are well kept and are relatively level to begin with, so this is typically not a huge undertaking. And, asphalt or concrete campsites are poured level. Note: Poured campsites are usually reserved for campers with disabilities. However, even as a camper qualified to use these sites, we seldom do. In the summer these sites just absorb the sun! It is like camping on a heating pad. If you do need to set up strictly on a poured site, try to find one in the shade. Otherwise, the surface you camp on makes no difference to your pop-up.

On the open ground, you might have to use a small 1"x6"x10" piece of board under one or more of the tires. My husband carries six or so of these boards for just this purpose.

The easiest way to level the camper is to place one or more of these boards in front of or behind your camper tire on the corner that needs raised and then drive up on them. Some people put them in front of the tire and drive up on them, but my husband just backs up on them into the place he wants to park the camper.

There are a couple of products on the market that make leveling your camper easy. By mentioning them, I am not necessarily endorsing them, I am just trying to give you information and options on things that apparently do work.

The first is a product called Lynx Blocks. These are interlocking blocks that can be arranged in a variety of configurations. They are made of heavy-duty orange thermo-plastic resin and all you do is stack the 8-1/2" x 8-1/2" blocks in a pyramid shape and drive your camper up onto them.

Luckily, my husband and I have never needed to stack the one-bys any higher than two to level our camper. I would imagine that if we had ever needed to stack the boards three or four high, they might have begun sliding when we tried to drive up on them. To help prevent this, saw the ends at a 45 degree angle. This will make them easier to drive up on without them sliding.

To prevent sliding, the ability of the Lynx block to stack into a pyramid shape would probably be very handy. I have read reviews on the blocks and most of the reviewers agree that the blocks do what they are designed to do and that two sets of ten were all these campers ever needed.

Another product receiving favorable reviews on the sites I have visited is the BAL Tire Leveler. With this product you park your trailer, place the leveler around the low-side tire and ratchet screw the device until your trailer is level. There is no need to drive your trailer back over or pull it forward to roll up on boards or blocks. You decide where you want to park and that is where you sit. This leveler is made of heavy-duty tubular steel.

After your camper is side-to-side level, insert the dolly wheel into jackpost and lock it in place. Lower the jack to ground. Unhook the safety chains. Raise the tongue with the jack until the coupler is free of the hitch. Move your tow vehicle out of the way. Use your tongue jack and level the camper front to back. When you have finished leveling, chock both in front of and in back of the wheels.

Some campers have a small two to three inch bubble level affixed to the side of the camper. Ours does not, so we store ours right inside the door of the camper in an easily accessible place.

Step Four ~ Unlatch the Roof: You are almost ready to raise the camper roof. Remember to unlatch yourthe roof latches! Forgetting to unlatch them can damage the lift system.

At this point, my husband gets his miniature bubble level out of the camper and really checks to see if the camper is, in fact, level. The best place to keep your bubble level, if one is not attached to your camper, is in a drawer immediately inside the door. That way you can just open the bottom half of the door on the camper and reach in to grab it - without raising the roof all the way just yet.

And you do not want to raise your roof all the way just yet if you have an awning. First you will want to complete Step Five - which I actually considered calling Step Four and One-Half.

Step Five ~ Unbag the Awning: If you have an awning, it is easier to unbag the awning and let down the poles while your roof is midway. You may have to angle the poles or raise them a couple of times before you have the roof completely raised. However, this is much easier than tippy- toeing to unzip your awning bag and pulling everything out when the roof is totally raised. If you are height challenged, like myself, tippy-toeing is not even an option. It is get a ladder or nothing, and a ladder is just something else to have to pack and lug along. Camper axles do have weight limits!

Remember, you want to set your awning poles uneven if you have AC or in case it rains. With one pole slightly lower than the other, the water and rain will run off of your awning - not make a huge pool of water in the middle that will bring your awning down on top of you water and all. (Ask my niece's husband just how shocking and cold an event this little shower can be!)

When tearing down, you will also want to stow your awning back in its bag while your roof is lowered midway. Lower your poles first! If you lower your roof without lowering your poles first, you run the risk of bending your poles or springing your roof out of shape.

Step Six ~ Get Cranking: It is time to totally raise the roof! My husband and I have almost always bought used campers, and one of the things he always checks is to make sure that the roof has not been raised over-much. On a lot of pop-ups there will be a guide wire on the front corner of your camper. When that wire is taut - not screaming tight - just taut, you have raised the roof enough. If there is not a guide wire there, find out why. Does the model camper you are looking at not have one or was the roof previously raised too high and the wire broke?

I have to admit, I can crank our camper up, but I am huffing and puffing before I am finished and I am no lightweight prima donna female, if you catch my drift...

Anyway, with that in mind I keep looking into a power lift to add onto our camper. Our camper does have the required tongue-mounted manual crank system for conversion with one particular model I have researched. But I have read mixed reviews. So, I am still cranking away. But not for long! For his birthday this year, my husband received a product called Socket Jenie. I had read multiple reviews and the consumers

wrote favorable comments about this product. Most all of them were pleased with the product. They did mention to make sure that you use a drill with enough torque to raise the roof and do the job. A 24 volt drill is recommended. My husband agrees.

Socket Jenie

Step Seven ~ Safety and Stability: Your camper is level, your awning is out, your roof is up. Now what? If your camper has roof safety supports to slide around the lift posts, now is the time to put them in place. Next, set your stabilizer jacks. Crank them or slide them down into place. My husband also carries four 2"x6"x6" blocks of wood on which to lower the jacks. This keeps our jacks clean, but more than that, if we happen to be on a "soft" campsite and it rains, our jacks do not end up settling into a mud pit.

It cannot be said too many times: The stabilizer jacks are for stabilizing only. They are simply to prevent your camper from rocking around when you are moving inside. They are not leveling systems! I repeat: They are not a leveling system! If you try to use the stabilizers as levelers, you can actually bend the frame of your camper by extending them too far. That is a costly and avoidable mistake.

Stabilizers are not for leveling!

They are for stabilizing only.

Step Eight ~ Secure the Awning: If your pop-up does not have anything to secure the awning with, go to you local discount store, meander back to the camping section and find some good sturdy metal (not aluminum) tent stakes and nylon rope. They do not have to be huge tent stakes, and the rope does not have to be much more than a quarter inch thick. But, this is a necessity!

After you have the awning set up, pound a tent stake into the ground at an angle away from one of the awning poles. The tent stake point will go in toward the awning, the end you are hammering will angle away. Once you have the stake in, tighten the ropes snugly.

When staking your awning, wrap the rope around the pole that comes out from the camper, as well as the pole that keeps the front stretched taut. You want your rope around both of these so that the wind does not move the rope back and forth and eventually do more harm than good to your awning. After you have the rope secured, pull it at an angle down to the ground and wrap it around your tent stake.

Remember, though, that one of your awning poles should be slightly lower than the other. By slightly, I mean a good four to six inches. Not only does this keep water from pooling on your awning should it rain, but keeping the end that is facing the prevailing wind a little lower, lessens the rustling and snapping your awning will do in a high wind.

Step Nine ~ Unpack Front Storage: Remove any items you know you will need from your front storage space if your camper is so equipped. You must especially remove any needed items if your storage space does not have a side access door. Fortunately, most models nowadays do have this door.

Step Ten ~ Pull Out Beds/Slideout: When you have retrieved your items from storage, close it back down and now you are ready to pull out the beds. Pull them out and put the supports underneath the beds in place. Do not pull your tenting around and under the beds just yet! Go inside the camper and put the bed bows in place. Now go back outside and pull your tenting around and under your bed and fasten it in place. If you remember my bivouac fiasco at the beginning of this section, you will immediately know why I maintain it is easier to put the bed bow in place with the tenting not pulled tight!

If you have a slideout or a bay window, now is the time to pull and/or push these out and secure their bows. Remove the screws, pull the room out, and secure the cotter pins. Go inside and place the bows before you start battening down your canvas.

Step Eleven ~ Lower the Door: Lower your door into position, align the twist holders on the upper portion, and make sure it opens and closes smoothly. Be careful and do not drop it and clunk yourself on the head. If your door does not open and close smoothly, there is a good chance your camper is not level. It is this very step that makes it important to actually level the camper in the beginning. It is much easier to level a camper prior to this stage.

Step Twelve ~ Hookup: I will admit that on hot and humid days, my husband puts step twelve before step ten. He has the electric hooked up and the air conditioning on before you can say, "It gets hot in Missouri in the summer!" But either way, now is the time to hook up to your electric and water if the campsite has it available. If your camper is a luxury model, and the campsite has drainage and sewer, pull out your grey and black water hoses and hook them up as well.

My husband and I used to own a pop-up with a shower/potti built in, but we have since traded for one with just a porta potti. While we had our "elite" camper, we used the shower in it exactly once. To us, it is just as easy to run up to the shower house to take our showers. Most shower houses are

conveniently located, and there is a lot less to
before lowering the camper. Plus, most pop
most, a six-gallon hot water heater and a tw
water holding tank. That is barely, and I do mean
enough for two adults to take two very, very short show
We do like the convenience of the porta potti, though.

Our present camper does not have a grey water tank
and we had to come up with something to catch our dirty sink
water. At first we used a simple five-gallon bucket. (You can
see this in the picture below.) My husband drilled a hose-sized
hole into the lid and we put the drainage hose down into the
bucket. This works just fine for short trips or once a day
emptying. We used this method for years.

I have seen some people just let their hose drain under
their camper. However, not only is this messy for the next
camper who pulls in on the site, it is definitely not ecologically
friendly. And, in most parks it is usually against regulations.

We now use a Tote Tank. They come in several
different sizes with two or four wheels. All you do when they
are full is attach them to your hitch and tote them to the dump
station. Ours is a two-wheel, fifteen-gallon tote and it works
great for two people over the course of a weekend.

Set Up and Ready to Play

Step Thirteen ~ Set Up Camp: You now have the _rdest_ part of pop-up camping finished. My husband and I _can_ usually complete the first twelve steps in less than one-half hour to forty-five minutes, if we are moving somewhat spritely; an hour or so if we are moving at a more leisurely pace. If it is pouring down rain, we can do those twelve steps in less than twenty minutes! Yup, I have timed us. We can move when there is inspiration to do so.

Step thirteen does usually move slower. On occasion, we have even stopped and fixed our supper or had a cooling adult beverage before completing step thirteen. Because step thirteen can last the entire trip. All you are doing in this step is making your camping trip as luxurious as you desire. Put out your awning lights or camping mats. Set up your outdoor grill if you have one. Organize the inside the way you prefer and enjoy your trip!

If you have just practiced raising your camper in your back yard, tearing down is basically everything in reverse. Note, some pop-up models specifically require you to latch either your front or rear latches first when your roof is down.

You cannot read the sign in the background, but it says, "Road Ends In Water." Ya think?

14

Read the Instructions Manual

Make sure you read your camper's instruction manual and learn whether your camper model has any special guidelines to consider in any of the set-up steps. Along that same line, be sure to read your camper's maintenance guide for specific maintenance schedules. There are helpful hints in them that are extremely useful.

Low Impact Camping or No Trace Camping

Every single one of the professionals who reviewed my manuscript told me that I could not place enough emphasis on the importance of taking care of the environment when camping. They all said, *"Pack it in. Pack it out. Respect it!" "Make as little impact on Mother Nature as possible."* They were passionate about this section of the book. They wanted everyone to embrace low impact camping. Let's do it!

They did thankfully agree that most of us do not have to go to the extreme I did on my best no-trace camping trip. That time was not only my best low-impact and no-trace camping trip, it was my wettest! I was doing escape and evasion survival training with the military and I ended up sleeping under a tree in my poncho in the pouring rain. I had successfully "moved toward friendlies" all day with my ruck, successfully kept myself hidden from the "enemy," and I was tired. It was pitch black and raining and I needed to sleep.

I crawled under a tree, laid my head back on my poncho hood, placed my helmet over my face so I would not drown in the rain, pulled my arms inside my poncho to try to keep somewhat warm and dry, and proceeded to eventually go to sleep. Sort of. I can honestly say that was the dreariest night I ever spent in the woods! But, hey, I was getting paid to be there, so why not? The scary part was when I awoke the next morning and realized I had snoozed in a patch of poison ivy. Yowza!

That is low impact camping! No fire, no tent, no nothing. Just me and Mother Nature, at her worst, I might add. Most of us will leave a little more impact with our stay in nature than I did on that occasion, but you never want your impact on nature to be more than it has to be. If you "take only pictures and leave only soft-soled footprints," Mother Nature will welcome you back with open arms the next time you are camping in her beautiful backyard.

A lot of people do not realize it, but the low impact camping philosophy is just as important to observe in a campground as it would be if you were hiking and camping in the "beyond the outback" part of the country. Perhaps even more so. Please let that sink in for a minute.

These areas get a lot of use. If everyone goes in with the attitude that "it's not really nature, so we don't have to worry about our treatment of it," then eventually - even that campground will experience ecological problems. Overuse accompanied by abuse can cause ravages that even Mother Nature will not be able to put right in a life time.

Some sources say there are seven principles to low impact camping, some say eight. Every source has a different number of principles to guide your low impact, leave no trace, camping trip. I say just remember to be G.R.E.E.N.

G.R.E.E.N. Considerations

Garbage In. Garbage Out: Always leave the campsite in better condition than you found it. If you packed it in, then pack it out. It is just that simple. And, truthfully, most people will try to collect their belongings and their garbage and get their garbage to a trash container. But, it never ceases to amaze me the number of cigarette butts, beer tabs, candy wrappers, and other small items that are invariably on any campsite that we have ever been on. This is trash too!

Maybe I was required to "police" the ole Army base one too many times while I was in the military. But when you have spent literally hours looking at the ground and picking up every tiny piece of trash some inconsiderate individual has tossed there, trust me, you do not throw anything on the ground!

If you are a smoker, "field strip" your butts. To do this, roll your cigarette butts around in your fingers, loosen the tobacco, let *that* fall to the ground to return to Mother Nature, and then put the butt in your pocket or in the trash where it belongs. It is not hard and soldiers have been doing it for as long as they have had cigarettes.

Those little candy wrappers and pieces of plastic need to go in the trash also. All that sugar on a tiny piece of plastic is irresistible to a critter, be it a squirrel or be it a raccoon.

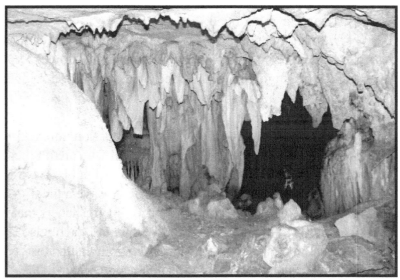

Visiting Springfield, Missouri, and riding through the sparkling Fantastic Caverns is a trip worth making summer or winter.

Unfortunately, that plastic can get stuck in their digestive systems and kill them. Dispose of all trash properly.

If there is anything you can recycle in your garbage, do so. We should all be cognizant of how each of us can best conserve our environment for future generations. We have already lost entire species of animals and flora, let's not add to that loss by abusing the nature we are enjoying.

Other than the fact that it is an eyesore, another reason to dispose of your garbage properly is its negative impact on wild animals. Entirely too many wild animals have had to be destroyed - (Isn't that such a nice politically correct euphemism?) ~ That means KILLED! - because the humans that were in the campsite continually left food scraps behind.

The result? The animals, especially bears, became expectant and somewhat reliant on those food scraps and became aggressive toward the humans camping. Bears have demolished tents, cars, and campers because they could smell food and have learned how to get to that same food we carelessly leave laying around.

If you are traveling in bear country, there are specially designed containers for food storage in which you should invest. These are highly recommended by Conservation Agents and Rangers who do not like to have to shoot a bear because someone has been thoughtless with food storage.

Dr. Case, who wrote my book's introduction noted, "In addition, if you travel to bear country, women who are on their period need to be careful hiking and plan accordingly." He was emphatic and serious about this subject. Bears have a great sense of smell! Any perfumes, colognes, or air fresheners that smell like vanilla and "berry this" or "berry that" might also attract unwelcome guests, not just bears, to your campsite.

Another negative result of people leaving their food and garbage outside or stored incorrectly, is that the animals fight for that food. Not only will they fight over the food, but in the process they will drag the food all over the campground.

Then a Park Attendant or Custodian has to be paid to clean it up. The campsite fees get raised and who pays? We do.

The container that any food was in also needs to be cleaned correctly and disposed of properly. If it is a can, burn it in the campfire to remove any remains of food even before you place it in the recyclable trash bin. If the food came in a jar, wash it when it is empty before putting it in the recyclable trash. Raccoons, especially, are liable to get their heads caught in a container when foraging for food. If their head gets stuck inside the container, they are in for a slow and agonizing death. It happens, and we can prevent it.

Lastly, do not bury your garbage. This is an old wive's tale that needs to go bye-bye. It does not work. Animals have a much better sense of smell than humans. They will simply dig it up and spread it around. They will thank you for the challenge of burying it - what a great game you provided - hide and seek and dig for my dinner - and animals love a challenge just like we do! So now you know, burying trash does not accomplish anything. Dispose of your trash properly.

One of the best day-hikes in Missouri is Elephant Rock State Park. Taum Sauk Mountain, the highest point in Missouri is close by. A fantastic campground, Johnson's Shut-In is nearby.

Respecting Mother Nature: I could really get on a soap box with this one, but I will endeavor to restrain myself. It is basically common sense. Do not mess with the animals. This means, do not feed the cute and cuddly-looking baby animal that is in the weeds beside the trail you are hiking. And do not try to pet the cute little furry baby animal. **Respect the Animals:** Leave the baby alone. Mama animal is probably somewhere very close and she will not appreciate your good intentions. To her, you are a threat to her child. Leave the baby animals alone. Leave the adult animals alone as well.

You will see several pictures of animals throughout this guide. They were all taken with a long zoom lens. I do not get close even when I can. With a zoom lens it is not necessary. I get my picture. Mama animal is not upset. Baby animal is not disturbed. It is a win-win picture situation.

It is a great experience to observe animals in nature in the wild. It is absolutely one of my favorite things to do. But, I abide by two very simple rules. I never approach an animal and I never feed an animal. I am not gong to contribute to changing anything about their behavior or feeding habits. I figure they know exactly what they need to do to survive in nature and they do not need my "human help" - translation - "interference."

Respect Plant Life: While you are respecting the animals, respect the earth and trees also. Do not pound a nail into a tree on your campsite to stretch a clothes line. After you are done chopping your firewood, do not slam your hatchet into a tree to "hang" it there until you are ready to use it the next time. All of those wounds can eventually cause the tree to die. Trees are resilient and amazing in their ability to withstand abuse, but they cannot survive repeated abuse. You may think, "well it is just one hole," but odds are it is not. Someone has probably already wounded that tree. Several someones, in fact. Your hole might just be the killing strike.

Stated simply, these seemingly small wounds cause stress to the tree that can result in an entry point for decay and over time they may eventually cause a vertical crack in the trunk. A tree trunk that has a vertical crack in it is an indication that the tree is dying. These spots also have the potential to become weak points in the tree.

If you are camping under a tree with one of these weak points, you may be the not-so-lucky recipient of a limb on top of your camper when the wind breaks it off. And, to think, it all started with just a few nail holes or hatchets buried in the tree trunk that did not need to be there. Do not strip bark off of any tree for any reason. Do not use small trees to tie clotheslines or tarps to. If you do use a large tree to tie a rope around, tie it loosely and remove it when you leave

Above: Damage done by a yellow nylon rope left tied.

Below: An abandoned chain has "girdled" this tree. Trees can die from girdling.

21

A bonfire, built entirely too big and way too close to this tree, caused this tree's trunk damage.

the campground! If left on long enough, the tree will grow around the item. This is called "girdling," and trees and branches do die from girdling.

Besides the clothes line to hang the bathing suit on, a campfire seems to be a necessity when camping. Some hard core "no tracers" will tell you not to make a fire at all. I will just say, do not light fires in places outside of an approved fire ring. If you are allowed a fire in an approved area, keep it small. I have seen some campers get darn near a bonfire going. Why? It is not necessary and it is a huge waste of our natural resources. And, do not venture into the woods around your campsite to cut down trees. Some sites do allow you to rummage for fallen dead wood, others do not. Make sure you know the regulations of your campground before you go rummaging. (You might also want to read the section on poison ivy prior to wood rummaging... Just a thought.)

Incidentally, do not burn your "household-type" of garbage. Burning household rubbish releases toxins into the atmosphere. Burn only dry, local, wood.

Respect Native Habitat: It is a good idea to buy your wood close to the campground. Do not bring a non-native wood to the campsite. You can bring disease and deadly pests to the local forest when you bring in non-native wood and you will not even realize the damage you have done.

Respect Native Species: Along those same lines, buy your bait locally. Do not bring non-native fish bait to use. Non-native species of fish bait may escape and displace native species. Alien species from other parts of the country will not have a natural predator to keep it at bay. In the absence of a natural predator, invading species can devastate native populations, their habitats, and whole ecosystems.

Bringing in a non-native species will always cause some change in the biodiversity of rivers and lakes. Usually the change is to the detriment of the very fish you are hoping to catch. One of Missouri's most unwanted alien species is the black-and-white striped Zebra Mussel. If you find this fingernail-sized mussel, contact the Conservation Department.

Anglers should dispose of unwanted bait on land or in the trash. Do not dump your bait bucket into the water as the water can contain invasive plant or aquatic species or disease microbes that are invisible to the eye. Angers should always clean their fish at approved and posted fish-cleaning stations.

Respect Fire: If you have started a fire, when you go to sleep or leave the campsite, put it out. Pour water on it so that it is totally extinguished. Other than the obvious safety hazards of an unattended fire - *please do not make me go there* - there is also the chance an unattended fire can start smoking excessively. You might not be there to care, but your neighbors in the next campsite will not appreciate being smoked out.

Okay, I *am* going to go there. Embers can escape from an unattended fire. Should those embers land on something and catch fire, you can end up with a disaster. It can be your tent or pop-up canvas that has caught fire. It can be the woods surrounding you that catch fire. Either way, it can all be avoided by simply extinguishing unattended fires.

Respect Rocks: This may seem too obvious to mention, but do not spray paint rocks or carve messages in tree trunks. No one cares you were there and Kilroy got old and retired after World War II.

Eco Friendly Considerations: Recycling has
already been mentioned, but there is another way to be ecologically friendly that we often fail to think about. Take advantage
of all the great new biodegradable products on the market.

I have seen some people at campgrounds washing their
dishes outside at the water pump. Not good, folks. No one
wants to step in your dirty dishwater when they are trying to
get clean water to take back to their campsite. Not to mention
that all those food crumbs will start smelling eventually. They
may also draw wild animals to the area - a subject we have
already covered previously.

Collect your grey water properly and take it to the
dumpsite. If you are at a primitive location, do not wash your
dishes in the lake or the stream. Gather your water in a bucket,
wash your dishes with your biodegradable soap, rinse, and
dispose of the grey water at least 150 to 200 yards away from
the clean water source if a dumpsite is not available. Spread
your grey water out when you are disposing of it. This allows
the water to filter through the earth before returning to the
clean water source.

If you have one of those solar showers, make sure you
are the same distance - 150 to 200 yards - from a natural water
source when showering. Also, always use bio-degradable
soaps and shampoos.

Etiquette for Campers: You do not need to
pollute the land and water, and you should not pollute the air
space. Remember, you are not the only one who has escaped
the city to get back to nature. While we would like to believe
that we are alone in our own little campsite communing with
nature, the truth of the matter is, we have neighbors and we
should be considerate of those neighbors. Campers and tents
have extremely light walls. Sound travels. Sound travels
exceptionally well in the wilderness and especially at night.

Add a lake of water and you can double how well sound will carry at night in the wilderness.

My US Army instructors told me over and over, again and again, "Sound carries at night. Sound especially carries at night in the wilderness." Uncle Army is right. I have heard entire conversations from some good ole boys five camp sites away who are smokin' and jokin', not to mention drinkin', late at night by the campfire.

Now I like a good joke and a frosty "adult beverage" right along with the best of them. And after spending twenty-five years in the military, I'll tell ya, some of those jokes I heard were beyond risque - but, I was in an environment where everyone there was on the same wave length.

Not so in a campground. The children in the next campsite really do not need to hear some of that language. I do not need to hear *some* of it! Not in that environment. Be courteous to, and be considerate of, your neighbors.

Remember to keep your voice down, and if you absolutely must have a radio or CD player on, keep the volume low and turn it off when you leave your campsite. It amazes me the number of people who leave their "boom box" blasting away in their absence. Many camping enthusiasts work in jobs and live in cities where they are surrounded by noise 24-7. Their dream is to have 72 hours on a weekend camping trip to actually hear birds chirping, leaves rustling in the trees, and silence. Yes, silence is golden to many.

Which means brings me to my "pet peeve." (Okay, I know, it is a bad pun.) But, here it is: Keep Fido quiet! My husband and I also have a dog and we have no problem taking him camping. He is a well-trained and wonderfully disciplined animal. So if he barks, I pay attention. It means something is wrong. Terribly wrong.

On the other hand, dogs that bark and bark and bark and bark and bark can drive a saint ballistic. Come on people, shut your dog up! It does not matter if it is the middle of the day and it isn't "quiet time." It is not necessary for a dog to bark excessively - and is actually a reflection of an unhealthy mental attitude on the part of your dog. Nobody wants to hear your dog yapping and yipping and barking his head off.

Personally, I do not want to hear your dog and I do not want to befriend your dog. Keep your dog on his leash. I do not care how friendly the mutt is, I do not want him in my campsite. I have my own dog, thank you very much. I really do not want to have another one. Not even for just a little campsite visit. Sorry. I guess I am just dog-anti-social.

I remember one camping trip where my husband and I were parked next to neighbors with a dog that they basically brought camping and then abandoned. They either leashed him to a tree all day while they were gone or they stuck him in his carrier twenty feet away from them while they sat at the picnic table laughing and eating and totally ignoring his constant irritating barking.

Saturday they decided they would leave him in their pop-up while they were gone all day, but they did not leave the AC on and it got hot! My husband and I were sitting under our awning when I saw something poke out of the neighbor's canvas at the corner of their pop-up. I told my husband to look and see if he saw what I saw. Sure enough. A couple of minutes later the dog poked his entire head out of the canvas. We kept watching and pretty soon the pooch escaped. He jumped out of the canvas all the way to the ground and ran around the campsite the rest of the day. Hubby and I looked at each other and said, "That can't be good." But we were both laughing as well. That pooch was determined to escape and he succeeded.

That evening my husband and I could hear the neighbors screaming when they returned. No exaggeration. Really screaming. Apparently the abandoned pup had ripped upholstery and canvas to shreds in their pop-up in his attempt to escape his hot prison. The moral of the story: If you cannot pay attention to your dog when camping, leave him at home.

My dog, bless him, has enough energy for two dogs. Honestly, you would think my dog was a racing grey hound or something! I lost ten pounds the first month I had him, just walking him! My husband named him "Champ," but I have called him "Diet!" I love our dog!

Anyway, I have to walk him a lot. He truly is a very energetic boy. And he poos a lot! So when I am walking him, I am carrying sandwich bags. I pick up poo. A lot of poo. I do not like stepping in it. I do not like smelling it. I for sure, do not want to deal with or step in someone else's dog's poo! Pick up your dog's poo. Many campgrounds, including Missouri State Parks, offer free "Doggie Poo Bags." When checking in at a camp ground, ask the Park Attendant if they have free "Doggie Poo Bags" and/or trash bags. If they do, take advantage of them. But, be prepared with your own stash as well.

Do not let your dog run free - not even when hiking on a trail. His curiosity could get him hurt, bit by a snake, or even attacked by another animal. Keeping your dog on a leash or in a portable pen is for his safety. In the picture below, I was more worried about our dog's nose than the turtle - it was a snapping turtle! Champ was fortunately smart enough to leave it alone and he was on his leash.

The Champ-meister investigating a turtle.

On a somewhat unrelated note, I think Israel has a great idea. When you take your dog to the veterinarian in Israel, the vet takes a sample of your dog's DNA. If you do not scoop up the poop, the poop police pick it up and send it in for DNA sampling. Then the doggy owner receives a fine for being a non-pooper scooper upper. How is that for taking this subject seriously! Yikes! I do wonder, though; do you think the fine is the same for a Toy Poodle as it is for a Great Dane?

By the way, I probably do not have to mention this, but, when you are walking your dog or just walking anywhere, do not walk through your neighbor's campsite. A campsite is such an extension of a pop-up or any camper that it is like walking though someone's house back home. Go around, please. Your neighbors will thank you.

The nice plus to keeping your dog quiet and the music volume down is that Mother Nature might reward you with a show of her wild animals. My husband and I have observed deer, wild turkey, Canadian geese, ducks, red and grey squirrels, shy little ground squirrels, all sorts of song birds, and a bobcat while quietly enjoying nature in our camp site. The connection with nature was magical.

Last, but not least, when you travel with your pets, be sure to keep their vaccinations up to date. Should the unthinkable occur and they are attacked by a wild animal, you will feel considerable relief knowing their vaccinations, especially their rabies shots, are current.

Never Say Never - Always Be Prepared: If something is going to happen, Murphy's Law says it will. I can happily say the military prepared me well for spending nights in the woods alone. They taught me to plan ahead and to always be prepared for the worst. And I am so glad they did. Because it seems whenever I say, "It'll never happen to me," Murphy says, "Wanna bet?" (Murphy is a pain in the ...) With Murphy in the picture, proper preparation can mean survival!

As an example; the time my husband and I went deer hunting one weekend at Truman Lake in Missouri, primitive camping was in order. We packed light that trip. We had our tent, our air mattress, two wool blankets, two cooking pots/ dishpans, a coffee pot/water bucket, two forks, and our hunting knives. We also had our rifles and ammunition, food, coffee, and fresh water, a battery operated lantern, and a little two-wheel pull cart to tote the gear into the woods and the deer out of the woods. We hoped, anyway.

Sunday afternoon my husband decided that he was going to go out and try one last time to get a deer. I told him that I would make a really big loop around the hill we were hunting and if there were any deer I would disturb them and maybe they would head his way and he could fill his tag. Well, I *thought* it was a good idea.

Unfortunately it did not turn out as planned. My husband's parting words to me were, "Don't get lost." Okay, does everyone remember Murphy? Why would my hubby tell me that? Guess what happened. I got lost. Really, truly, bona fide, could not find my way out of the woods, lost. Oh, did I mention that an ice storm was expected to move in that night?

Fortunately, I was prepared. I had my hunting knife, I had my rifle, I had my lighter, and I was dressed warmly in multiple layers. After walking for hours on end, I decided to bed down for the evening. I found a nice area out of the wind and started a small fire. I was nice and cozy when I heard a car horn honking. Yahoo, I am saved!

I jumped up, put out my fire, and headed toward the sound of the horn. But wait, the stupid horn kept moving. I would head toward it, and hopefully out of the woods, and it would move and I would have to change directions. That was not good. So I gave up on the horn and headed back to my little campsite. Did I mention that it was dark as can be, heavily overcast, and cold as a witch's you know what? And, don't forget the ice storm in the forecast...

Anyway, I had not made it even half the way back to my campsite when I heard another horn. I was not getting fooled twice. I stood there in the dark and listened very carefully for about fifteen minutes for that particular horn to move. It didn't. It stayed stationary so I headed for it.

I eventually came to a dirt access road. Remembering the other horn moving every few minutes, I started running up this dirt road toward the sound of the horn. Little did I know there was a three-quarters inch wire cable stretched across the road waist-high about fifty feet from the black top road where the vehicle was parked and honking. Remember me mentioning how dark it was? I darn near hung myself running into that *%#)&(-@ bleepity-bleep cable in the dark.

I hit that cable, did a soaring gold-medal Olympic-qualifying somersault, flipped over the cable, and landed flat on my back with the wind totally knocked out of me. I can laugh about it now, but at the time all I could think of when I was laying flat on my back staring up at the sky and literally gasping for air, was Wiley Coyote in the cartoons. I now knew exactly how he felt when he fell off of a cliff and went splat.

Primitive camping at Truman Lake.

(Before being lost.)

Check out all the different camo patterns. Am I "styling" or what?

After I recovered, I pulled myself up and headed for the vehicle that was still honking. Bless that searcher's heart and all searchers everywhere, canine and human alike. I found out they had the Sheriff's department, all the volunteers they could muster, the Highway Patrol, and the Water Patrol out looking for me. They had dogs from another county on the way. I think they were all very happy that I knew how to survive and that I walked out unhurt - well, except for almost flipping myself silly, a story I did not tell anyone but my husband until now.

On the flip side (aargh, what a painful pun), that was absolutely the best excuse I ever had for not going to work that Monday morning. It is 0800 hours and I am calling in to my office: "Uh, Colonel Jameson, this is Lieutenant Allee. I am not going to make it in to duty today. Why? Well, Steve and I went hunting this weekend and I got lost in the woods last night and I am just now getting home. I have been awake all night trying to find my way out of the woods. Yes, really! They had the highway patrol, water patrol, sheriff's department, and volunteers out searching for me."

Yup, you can imagine his reaction. A hearty guffaw does not quite describe it. And, bless his heart, when I did make it in to duty on Tuesday, my Colonel and my coworkers (whom he had apparently told the story to with great glee) had placed a compass and a map on my desk. Wasn't that sweet of them? I heard about that incident right up until I retired fifteen years later.

And, honestly, up until the point where I got lost, my husband and I were having an excellent time. We were deep in the woods around Truman Lake in Missouri, far, far away from civilization, camping in the great outdoors, leaving little to no trace behind, and communing totally with nature. I do not regret that trip at all. Not even getting lost.

Oh! The Sheriff questioned my husband about my disappearance. When my husband told me that I hee-hawed!

I know the Sheriff was just doing his job - and it is so sad he had to consider that option. I am just glad I am happily married to a man who loves his crazy-for-camping wife.

But anyway, this last note on low impact camping is simple. If you are not actually experienced in and prepared for primitive and back-country camping (which is an entirely different book), stay on designated "day hike" trails when hiking. Stay "found," and always be prepared.

I shudder to think of the possible consequences of being lost had I not been Army trained and prepared. In a nutshell, camping enthusiasts staying close to campgrounds and practicing low impact camping just need to remember to be **G.R.E.E.N.**

Garbage in. Garbage out.
Respect Mother Nature
Eco Friendly Considerations
Etiquette for Campers
Never Say Never -
      Always Be Prepared!

Camping under the pavilion, out of the rain.

Chapter Two
~ Soup ~
Plan Your Trip

What Goes in the Mix?

Planning and preparation for every trip is different. Are we boating? Are we fishing? Are we skiing? Are we hiking? The questions are endless and the preparation is different. I became most aware of the necessity of prior planning on a tent camping and bicycling trip on the Katy Trail that crosses a good half of Missouri: four days, three nights, and 225 miles.

Our pup tent, our sleeping bags, our clothes, food, water, bicycle tools, and spare parts, were all strapped on our bicycles. We had a blast! Each of our bicycles weighed over 100 pounds when packed and our thigh muscles got quite a workout, but it was so worth it!

We took that trip with our pastor and his wife and I can honestly say it was one of the best camping vacations my husband and I have ever taken. There are several campgrounds

That innertube was a lifesaver!

along the Katy Trail to stay at and in two of the towns that did not have campgrounds, they were willing to let us stay underneath their city park's pavilion. (We asked first. We did not just barge in and set up camp. If something had been scheduled for the pavilion, we did not want to interrupt.) In the end, we were very thankful for that generosity on the part of one particular town since one of those nights it poured down rain. Lots of rain. We were high and dry, though, underneath the pavilion.

With plenty of towns along the way, if you get tired of your packed food (we had MREs, which are military Meals Ready to Eat), there are several restaurants to take advantage of for a few meals. We had purchased *The Complete Katy Trail Guidebook* by Brett Dufur in advance of our trip, so we were well prepared for every leg of our trip. I read the book!

If you ever have a chance to cycle the Katy Trail, I highly recommend doing so. I also recommend you strap a riding lawnmower tire innertube to your bike seat for the comfort factor of your bottom's endurance test. Otherwise, if you are a tendertoosh (like me), you will not be able to enjoy the beautiful country and wildlife in abundance on the trail.

This trip drove home to me the necessity of planning each trip, every time - even if we are going to the same ole campground. For efficiency's sake, the education learning curve, and the pure pleasure of camping in the great outdoors, I am glad we started with tents. But I still love my pop-up best (and with my book, you can skip the tent learning curve. Yay!)

Who is Going and How Experienced Are They?

When we were planning our Katy Trail bike trip with our pastor and his wife, we were new to the idea of camping without a motor vehicle nearby. It was actually kind of a scary thought! Even with all of the camping my husband and I had done, we did not know what to expect. We were, to some extent, stepping out into new territory.

However, we were comfortable with the company we would be keeping. Our pastor and his wife were avid camping enthusiasts and knew exactly how to pack lightly. My husband and I were experienced campers with good survival skills.

But, it is definitely worth the time to consider who your camping companions are going to be on every trip. You will be in close proximity for hours on end. Even in a public campground with plenty of diversions, good questions to ask yourself are:

Does your friend have any outdoor abilities at all?

Is your friend active or sedentary?

Will he or she help around the campsite or sit and watch you do all the work?

Is your friend bringing another friend?

Is *that* person someone you want to be in close proximity to for the entire camping trip?

Is the person a positive or a negative individual?

Do I want to camp with a group or get away from it all?

Think about it. My husband and I love each other dearly - and after twenty years together, we know what gets on the other's nerves. But note: "Getting close" and enjoying each other's company can quickly change to "getting crowded" and on each other's very last nerve if we are not in harmony! I guarantee any issue we are having in our relationship is amplified when we go camping! It will be that way with every one of the individuals in your camping group. Make sure you actually like the people you are going camping with!

Children

Children are a special consideration as well. How old are they? Baby, toddler, child, tween, or teen? What specific gear do you need for them? How will you keep them entertained? If you plan on going on a day hike, does the trail accommodate strollers or will you need a child carrier?

My niece and my daughter-in-law (DIL) both love pop-up camping. I have a seven year old grandson who has camped since he was a baby and a great-niece and two great-nephews who have also camped since they were young'uns. When I asked my DIL and niece their best idea for camping with little children, they both gave me the same advice.

Have a plastic tub or a five-gallon bucket that is filled with toys that are age appropriate. Do not let the children play with these toys except when they are camping! It makes these toys "special" and they are amused by them longer, since they know they only get to play with them while the pop-up is up! Every year before the first camping trip, my DIL and niece go through the toys to upgrade to the new age of the children.

I have also seen campers with a small tent set up on the campsite with all the kids and toys inside. I thought it was an innovative idea. The tent made a great play pen and you could tell the toddlers thought it was absolutely and totally "cool" to be playing in their own tent. It is also a good idea to tie bright ribbons around trees to mark the boundaries of where young children are allowed to run and play.

My tween to teen great-nieces are beyond toys. They spend their time at the swimming beach or riding their bicycles around the campground. Since their parents cannot watch over them 100% of the time with these activities, my great-niece has a walkie-talkie she carries with her at all times. If she has a flat on her bicycle or any other problem, help - in the form of Mom or Dad - is within walkie-talkie distance. Just do not leave the spare batteries back at the camp site!

Seniors

At the other end of the age spectrum, my husband and I have camped regularly with his parents, his sister and family, and my mother. Fortunately, we are all in good shape and enjoy these camping excursions. But, his parents and my mother did and do have to remember to bring their required medications. If we are going to be gone for more than a couple of days, they have to make sure they will have enough for the entire trip or get a refill before we leave.

There is actually quite a nice thing about camping with other adults along. More adults means there are more people to share the workload and the costs. When camping with my entire family, my mother and I almost always do the evening cooking. My mother-in-law and sister-in-law almost always do breakfast. It is a great arrangement because I am not a morning person. I am a night owl. On the other hand, my mother-in-law and sister-in-law are up with the sun.

Where Are We Going?

Travel to and from the camp site is another consideration when planning a camping trip. My husband and I usually leave sometime on Friday afternoon or evening. I have a small cooler packed with snacks and drinks and am ready to go when he arrives home. That way we do not have to stop on the way to eat. We can hook up and go.

A lot of times we have pulled into the camp site right at dark. We try to be a good neighbor and quietly set up camp without making too much racket. Hopefully we succeed. We have slept in the truck when we have arrived in the wee hours and then just set up the next morning. Once, we even pulled onto a gravel road right off the highway somewhere and popped up the camper to sleep in. I still do not know where we were on that particular occasion.

Travel time to the camp site is a major consideration when planning a camping trip. Remember to include Murphy in your plans. He has a nasty habit of showing up when least expected and he is most unwelcome!

What Rules Apply?

Like most people, my husband and I are creatures of habit. Many times we travel to the same spots over and over. We have one favorite campground that is within a two hour drive of our home town where we probably camp four out of five times a year.

This particular campground has the advantage of having several campsites. Which means, unless it is a holiday weekend, we can almost always find an empty site. It has three shower houses, laundry facilities, and several other amenities we just like to have available when camping.

It is also convenient. We do not have to make big plans to go camping. Anytime during the summer that we decide we can take a couple of days and escape, we head to this same campground. We do not have to make huge plans. We can leave on a Friday evening after work and come back home on Sunday afternoon. In the meantime we have had a great weekend away from the phone and television. We truly commune with nature and each other.

Who Knows Where You Are Going?

Always file a trip plan with family members or friends so they know where you are going and when you are expected to return. While nothing may happen on your trip, something may happen back home while you are gone. Someone needs to know where you went and how to contact you. Most campsites have a Camp Host with a telephone land line for emergencies where there is no cell phone reception. Ask for that number.

When my husband and I are planning a trip to a new area, I try to get on the internet and gather as much information as possible about the campgrounds available. For the purpose of visiting a new vacation spot, I developed a Campground Checklist.

Campground Checklist

What is the weather expected to be like?

What campgrounds are close to our destination?

Are they Kampgrounds of America (KOA), Woodall's or Good Sam Club affiliated campgrounds?

Are there State Parks or U.S. Army Corps of Engineer Parks available to take advantage of?

Is a gate locked at night?

How do we get out at night in case of emergency?

Are we going to stay in a privately owned park?

What are the costs?

Do we have to pay for a minimum number of days?

If we have to cancel, do we still pay?

May we reserve a site in advance?

Are the sites pre-assigned?

Can we choose our own site when we arrive?

Is there a particular time to check in/check out?

How close are the campsites?

Are they under shade trees?

Are campsites dirt, grass, gravel, asphalt, or cement?

>   (Asphalt or cement sounds nice, but unless it is shaded, it can become a hot heating pad in the summer time!)

Do the campsites have electricity at the very least?

Do they have a water hook up?

Is there a sewer hook up or dump station?

What are the rules of each campground I am researching?

Are pets allowed? Is a leash required?

Do they have "silent times" after a certain hour?

Is there more than one shower house?

Do we need quarters to turn on the shower?

>   (Ever been naked in a shower stall with no quarters? Hmmmh.)

Need dimes for the toilet?

>   (I am not kidding! I have been in a restroom where you needed a dime to open the stall doors. It still flabbergasts me.)

Are laundry facilities available?

Is there a pool or a swimming beach?

Is there a lifeguard ever on duty?

Are there playgrounds and play equipment?

Are they metal or plastic?

> (Metal slides can burn a child
> if they are in the hot summer sun!)

Are there any entertainment facilities?

Is there a "little store" for basic necessities?

Is breakfast offered? If so, how much? What time?

How many vehicles may we park on our site?

May friends tent camp with us on our site?

Does it cost extra for them to do so?

Is there a boat dock?

Where do we have to park the boat?

Is there security?

Does a park ranger or a county sheriff make rounds?

Are areas designated and campfires allowed?

If no campfires, may we bring and use a fire pit?

Are fireworks allowed on the Fourth of July?

If your cell phone does not get reception,
  is there a land line for emergencies?

What shelters are available in the facility
  in case of severe weather?

Is there a severe weather warning system in place?

Do I have a Weather Radio with fresh batteries packed?

Those are the basic questions I like to have answered prior to embarking on a trip. You many have others. So I have provided plenty of blank space for you to add your questions.

_____

_____

_____

_____

_____

_____

_____

_____

_____

_____

_____

_____

_____

_____

_____

_____

_____

_____

_____

_____

_____

_____

_____

Your questions may also vary some according to what you plan to do recreationally on your trip. Hopefully, though, these basic questions will get you started. Many campgrounds have websites or toll-free 800 numbers. Call or log on to those websites and most of your questions should be answered.

What Kind of Weather is Expected?

This is the first question on my campground checklist and maybe the absolute most important! Fortunately, my husband and I are usually prepared for any and all types of weather we may encounter. Especially since we got stranded one time on Truman Lake.

That particular time my husband, his cousin, and I were fishing on Truman Lake in Missouri. It was a beautiful autumn day. The sky was a brilliant blue and puffy white clouds floated peacefully above us. Just beautiful!

The next thing we knew we were surrounded by fog. It was only about 4:00 in the afternoon. Talk about surprised! This was not a light fog either. This was the kind of fog that moves in and hovers so thickly that water begins dripping from tree branches and it sounds like it is raining, but it is not. It is just the fog dripping.

There we were trapped in fog in the middle of Truman Lake in an old John boat. There was no way we were making it back across the lake to the dock and home that night. My husband slowly and carefully guided the boat to a cove he had spotted earlier. It had to be slowly and carefully, because Truman has a lot of dead trees under water in its coves. You do not want to be going fast when you head into one of Truman's coves!

We made it to shore and prepared to settle in at our unexpected campsite for the night. Now what you have got to keep in mind is that we were fishing - not camping. Needless to say, we did not have any camping gear with us. And none of the three of us were cigarette smokers, so we didn't even have a lighter with us. We were wet and cold and we needed to start a fire before hypothermia set in. Hypothermia can set in at 50 degrees Fahrenheit and we wanted no part of it.

My husband's cousin attempted the Indian trick of rubbing two relatively dry sticks together. I do have to give him credit, he did get smoke. After almost an hour! He never did get fire. I tried to find a flint striker in our tackle boxes with no luck. (You can bet there is one in each of them now!)

My husband said, "I'll get a fire going." Oh, boy. That thought struck fear in my heart! First of all, hubby dearest is something of a pyromaniac. I think all men are secretly. It goes back to cave man days and barbecue grills, or something. I don't know. Anyway, the next thing I know, my hubby has the boat's battery out and on the bank where we are planning on starting a fire to keep us dry and warm. He hooked up a couple of pieces of wire to the battery, knocked them together and got sparks. Sure enough, after a couple of tries, he had a fire going. How innovative!

We made it through the night and actually kept fairly warm. We used our life preservers as pillows and I hid under my rain poncho to keep the fog from dripping on my face. I used a white trash bag as a "pillow case" over the top of a life preserver I used as a pillow. In spite of our rocky mattress, all in all, we did pretty good. The next morning the sky was again a brilliant blue, the sun was shining, and the fish were biting. It ended up being a great trip.

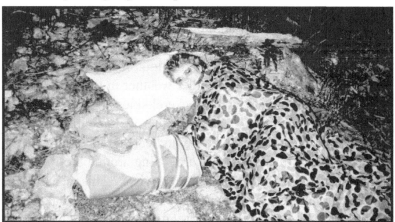

Stranded and sleeping on the rocks. My pillow-case is a white trashbag over a seat preserver.

But you need to know if bad weather is expected. Perhaps you can schedule your trip for another weekend. If you are locked into a particular weekend and bad weather is expected, preparation can ensure your trip is enjoyable regardless. And, watching the sky and clouds can help if you have some basic knowledge to go by.

Watching the Sky

There are several old sayings concerning the weather and each of them have some semblance of the truth in them. The old sailor's saying, "Red sky at night: sailor's delight. Red sky at morning: sailor take warning," has a great deal of truth to it. And sailors have been saying this for literally centuries!

Re: Bible verses, Matthew 16:2-3, which read, "When it is evening, you say, *It will be* fair weather, for the sky is red. And in the morning, *There will be* a storm today, for the sky is red and threatening." (New American Standard Bible)

There really is a scientific reason for these colors. Weather typically travels from the west to the east. Dry weather in the west means there are more dust particles floating in the air. The "red sky at night" is caused by the sunset's rays filtering through those dust particles. The dry weather from the west will be your dry weather the next day.

"Sun dogs," colored arcs that look like mini rainbows in the air, are a good sign of cooler weather in the future. There is another old saying, "Mackerel skies and horse's tails make tall ships carry low sails." In other words, cirrus clouds (which resemble equine tails) may indicate an incoming storm.

At night time when you are sitting around the fire, look at the smoke. Does it rise aloft in thin wisps? This means you are under a high-pressure weather system and continuing good weather for your camping trip. If your smoke stays close to the ground as it rolls away, you are camping in low-pressure weather and this may mean rain is on the way.

Clouds

Monitor the clouds. They do tell a story. Pay close attention when they are beginning to multiply. And take special note if they start getting lower to the ground. Bad weather might follow.

There are three main types of clouds. The first one is cumulus clouds. These are the clouds that look like big puffy cotton balls. If they are a bright white and high in the sky, and mostly horizontal in shape, you can usually count on good weather. If they are dark and low, and are stacking on top of themselves vertically, then prepare for some thunder, rain, and lightning. Note, conditions can change rapidly.

Cumulus Thunderhead

Stratus clouds are thinner and horizontal. These are the clouds you will usually see on a hazy day and typically, they are simply the above-ground fog that formed when cold air was moving in. They do not usually bring rain or storms other than a light mist or a drizzle.

The third main type of cloud is the cirrus cloud. These clouds are bright white, wispy looking clouds and generally indicate fair weather. They have the nickname, "mare's tails." Like all clouds, though, if they darken and descend lower in the sky, they can bring rain.

There are several other cloud variations, but these three types are usually present to some degree or other. If the clouds are moving rapidly across the sky, and temperatures are dropping, look for weather conditions to change rapidly.

A fourth type of cloud, the nimbus, has no definite shape, but is a low mass from which precipitation is currently falling or will shortly be counted on to fall.

Stratocumulus

Changing Weather

Heavy dew on the grass in the morning means you will have good weather for the rest of the day. If the grass is dry in the morning and the sky is hot and "close" feeling, then a storm is probably on the way. A "halo" around the sun or moon means rain within a day or so in the summer.

High Winds

With a pop-up, one of the first weather things to consider is high winds. Make sure your roof braces are in place. They are not just for looks, they will help keep your roof from swinging too far in a high wind. My husband and I have been camping in 50-60 mph winds and our camper has done just fine. But, we always make sure we practice safety first. Our roof braces are always in place. Always.

Cirrus

If you have an awning, you might want to consider putting it away in high winds. If not, make sure you have the poles staked securely into the ground. Not one of the pop-ups my husband and I have owned have ever had ropes or stakes in the awning bag to do this with. And we have watched awnings fly "up and over" because the owners did not know to or did not take time to stake their awning poles.

Thunderstorms and Lightning

If a thunderstorm blows in, get inside your camper or, better yet, go to the showers or the designated place for shelter. Avoid open spaces and do not sit outside to watch the storm. Thunderstorms frequently bring hail. If the hail is large enough, you can be seriously injured if struck.

Do not stand under a tree in a lightning storm. Lightning is attracted to the tallest object in an area and can travel under the ground to where you are standing.

I have a friend who was struck by lightning and he kept saying, "What are the odds?" Actually, the odds are about

Nimbostratus

one in 600,000, but he was the one. It would have helped if he had not been standing under a lone tree in an open area. This is one of the worst places to stand. A lone tree in an open place is very apt to be hit! My friend would have been better off in a stand of trees fairly even in height and a good distance away from any water. If you cannot be in a proper shelter, the best place to be during lightning is close to the ground.

Hail and Tornadoes

A hail storm occasionally precedes a tornado. If the sky turns a dark "green" color, again, get to your campground's storm shelter. Do not stay in your camper. Do not stay in your travel vehicle. If your campground does not have a designated storm shelter, lie flat in a ditch or depressed area and cover your head with your hands. Most tornado-related fatalities and injuries are caused by flying debris. Be aware that a tornado may be accompanied by flash flooding if a large amount of rain has fallen. When resorting to a ditch or depressed area for cover, keep this in mind.

Cold Weather Camping

With all the weather variety, camping in the fall is my favorite time of the year to camp. Can I say that again? I love camping in the fall! The crowds at the campground are almost nonexistent and the campfire at night really has a purpose. The nights get cool. Before my husband and I had our current Flagstaff pop-up that has a furnace, none of our previous pop-ups were so equipped. Not to worry, though.

Find a small ceramic heater in your local discount store and take it along with you. These little heaters will warm up a pop-up in the morning just fine. And they are tiny! They are perfect to store in a pop-up. Ours is about 7"x7"x4" sized. That is pop-up size! Plus, they can crank out a lot of heat. My husband and I have actually had to turn ours down when it got too hot in the pop-up! In addition, some of them have a wonderful safety feature. If they turn over, they turn off. However, since they sit so close to the ground, you almost have to purposely knock them over for them to actually turn over. That is a nice safety feature.

Do not use your cooking stove for heating purposes! This is a dangerous, even deadly, practice. Do not do it. You can asphyxiate yourself. Just get a ceramic heater. They are small and very cost efficient. We bought ours for less than $20.00 and I do not think the price has gone up on them much at all, if any, over the years. Along those same lines, do not use a kerosene heater in your pop-up! These heaters are not made for the small enclosed space of a pop-up. You are just asking for serious trouble. Deadly trouble. Do not do it.

Staying warm in a pop-up with a ceramic heater in moderately cold weather is easy. Add another sweater or a sweatshirt, throw on an extra pair of socks, and I guarantee most of you will be toasty warm!

As a matter of fact, my husband and I used to have two of these little heaters in our camper that did not have a furnace. We eventually cut back to the one. Two was too many. We actually got hot! Unless you are camping in the extreme cold, one ceramic heater will be more than sufficient.

A little ceramic heater and a portable weather radio are easily stored in an out of the way cubby hole in a pop-up. (The radio is out of sight in this photo.)

Layering Clothing for Cold Weather

When cold, the body will preserve the function of the heart and the brain by constricting blood vessels in the peripheral circulation. Areas most vulnerable to cold weather injury are the fingers, toes, ears, nose, and, for males, the penis. These areas will need extra care to stay warm and dry.

Layering your clothing in cooler weather helps to ensure you do stay warm and dry. Several layers of lightweight clothing are preferable to one thick layer of clothing. When wearing several layers, if you get too warm, you can remove a layer. Get too cold, pull a layer back on.

You do not want to sweat in your clothing in cold weather. Two things happen. First, your clothing becomes damp and the insulating value of the clothing is hampered. Second, as the sweat evaporates on your skin, your body cools. It is imperative you stay dry in cold conditions.

Wear your clothing loose. If the clothing, or your footwear, is too tight it will restrict blood circulation and invite a cold injury, such as frost bite. Also, the air between the loose layers is a thermal warming area.

Layer One: When layering, the first layer is your intimate underwear. In cold weather do not wear cotton underwear. If you do perspire, it will stay damp. Go for synthetic undies and wool socks. Wool socks are the best!

Layer Two: A second layer might be long underwear if you are camping in really cold weather. Make sure your long underwear is capable of "wicking." This means that the article of clothing is capable of "wicking" or "pulling" your perspiration away from your body.

If your long underwear does not have this capability, as your perspiration turns to ice, you will end up colder than if you had no long johns on at all. Even worse, you could get hypothermia, a deadly condition in which the body's temperature cools to 95 degrees Fahrenheit or below.

And, note, it does not have to be freezing outside for you to get hypothermia! This is a huge misconception! I have mentioned this once, but it deserves a second mention. The temperature can be as balmy and moderate as 50 degrees Fahrenheit and hypothermia can become a threat. If you are inadequately clothed, perhaps wet, or stay out long enough, your body temperature can drop below 95 degrees - and that is dangerous. Do not take the threat of hypothermia lightly.

A common "Rule of 50" says, "If you are cold and wet for more than 50 minutes in weather that is less than 50 degrees, you have a 50-50 chance of survival when suffering from hypothermia." That said, back to layering clothes.

Layer Three: The third layer consists of your normal clothes. These clothes should draw the moisture from your second layer to help your body stay warm. Good fabrics to choose for this layer are wool or quick-drying synthetics. Fleece is also a good choice as it has a great ability to keep you warm. Cotton is not. It is best to not wear cotton at all in cool and cold weather. It will soak up any moisture and retain it. Cotton takes a long time to dry in cool conditions.

Layer Four: Your fourth layer of clothing is your outer wear. This is your coat or your rain gear. Whatever is actually keeping the elements away from your body. My favorite outer wear fabric is Gore-Tex. It is somewhat expensive, but worth it. Gore-Tex allows perspiration to escape to the outside, so your inner clothes stay dry while keeping rain out.

Years ago I bought a Gore-Tex rain suit for my husband to hunt in, and it is still in great shape. He complained of the cost at the time, but I told him it was cheaper than him being treated for the flu or pneumonia that he might catch when he is out sitting in a deer stand in all kinds of weather! One really cold and rainy hunting season later, he finally agreed with me.

Do not forget gloves or mittens. Mittens keep your hands warmer, but you do sacrifice dexterity.

Layer Five: In extremely cold weather, a parka goes over everything. This is also the layer where you wear mittens over your gloves. If you are camping in weather that needs this layer, you need to be reading a survival book!

Sizzling Summer Heat

Obviously I have covered the worst weather first. But, truly, most of us camp in the summer. It is hot. It is muggy. And, it is a great time to get a sun tan. Or a sun burn. Or a heat injury.

Do not mess around with your health in hot weather. If you get cramps in your abdomen or limbs, sit down, rest, and rehydrate. If you get a headache, have dizziness, or feel nauseous; again, get out of the sun, sit down, rest, drink water, and cool off.

If you suspect heat stroke, a serious condition where the body temperature may climb to dangerously high digits, seek medical help immediately. Try to cool down by applying water-soaked cloths to exposed skin and by fanning yourself.

When it comes to sunburns, do not mess with skin cancer. Get a good sunscreen and use it. Make sure you reapply according to the instructions on the bottle. Sunscreen does not last forever or even through a whole day. Reapply generously and often. Do not forget the following areas: Your nose, the tops of your ears, the tops of your feet, the back of your legs, the back of your neck, and your shoulders.

Wear sunglasses. Wear a hat. And, on occasion, you might even want to wear a light-weight, light-colored, long-sleeved shirt. If you are going to be out in the blazing sun all day long, you might seriously consider a long-sleeved shirt. Your arms will appreciate your thoughtfulness. At the very least, wear a tee-shirt and not a tank top in order to protect the tops of your shoulders.

Also - you can sunburn just as bad, if not worse, on cloudy days as you can on sunny days. Use sunscreen on cloudy days as well!

When at all possible, stay in the shade, take plenty of rests, and drink water. Drink water even if you are not thirsty. Taking a lot of small drinks over a long period of time is more effective than drinking a huge amount all at once. Urine should be somewhat clear and no darker than straw. And please take time to eat!

I gotta tell ya. The only time in my entire military career that I succumbed to heat injury and flat passed out, I had been drinking water like a fish all day. What I had not done was eat. I told myself, "It is too hot. I'm not hungry."

When I awoke with an IV stuck in me, my commanding officer was ready to chew me up and spit me out for not drinking my water. Lucky for me, when he started bellering, "How many times did I tell everyone to drink water! I told you to drink plenty of water!" I could say, "I did, Sir! Like a fish! Sir. But, I'm afraid I didn't eat." I was over-hydrated, a serious medical condition called hyponatremia.

Now it is never too hot for me to eat! So when you are reading all the wisdom about drinking water to stave off heat injuries, remember to eat also! All that water flushes critical electrolytes out of your body. You body needs the electrolytes in the food, too. And, while there are a lot of drinks out there advertising "electrolytes," they are not a do-all and prevent-all solution. Eat. Drink. Enjoy.

 Our niece, "Princess Di," just waking up. Notice the shelf behind her. This pop-up accessory is one of our favorite and most convenient addition extras.

Chapter Three
~ The Salad ~
What Is In a Pop-Up?

After a couple of years tent camping, we moved "up" to our first pop-up camper (pictured on page 4). It was a little Palomino Pony. It might have been small, but it was cozy. It contained an ice box (no, not a refrigerator, an ice box) and to get water from the tank into the sink we had to use a hand pump. There was not an electric water pump.

There was electricity for the lights and propane for a two burner stove. There was no air conditioning, no furnace, and no water heater. But, it was easy to keep packed and ready to go between trips. It did not blow away in the wind and we could sit inside at the dinette and play cards on nights when the mosquitoes were just deadly.

We bought our starter pop-up camper used for around $1,500.00, way less than any camping trailer or motor home we have ever looked at. That little camper probably did not weigh much over 2,200 pounds fully loaded and was very easy to pull down the road behind our van. Because of a pop-up's ability to "fold down," there is not a huge profile to catch a lot of wind either. They pull much easier, do not get buffeted so much by a passing semi-trailer, and to some extent, I think this makes them safer to pull than a larger camping trailer.

I also feel safer with a locked door between me and the great outdoors. I can leave my camper locked and go on day trips without worrying about hiding my gear. Granted, theft in campgrounds is extremely rare, but it does unfortunately happen. I like having the ability to lock my camper with my gear inside. No, it will not keep out a determined thief since the ends are made of canvas just like a tent, but the lock does at least provide a deterrent.

A couple of years after my husband and I purchased the Palomino we decided to upgrade and we bought a Flagstaff. We had air conditioning, an electric water pump, a water heater, a three-way refrigerator, and a porta potti. We had a small ceramic heater to ward off the cold on chilly nights. Now we were camping! We had all of the comforts of an RV, without a huge bank loan.

We worked our way up to a Coleman with a built in shower and toilet (surrounded by a curtain) and thought we were at the top of the heap pop-up camper wise. However, as I have already mentioned in Chapter One, we used the shower only once in two years. It simply is not that big of a deal for us to slip on some shower shoes and head to the shower house that is available at most campgrounds where we camp. Plus, using the shower house means I do not have to clean and dry a shower out before we close the camper down.

We soon decided we were not real happy with Coleman's "one-piece" roof. After we added an air conditioner on top, the roof sagged in the middle. Apparently a lot of them sagged, because Coleman has since quit manufacturing that particular roof.

This was about the time that we decided to try a full-size hard-sided camping trailer. We were able to purchase a very nice twenty-eight foot trailer for a reasonable amount of money. It had a queen-sized bed in the bedroom and a good sized bathroom with a real door to shut when in use. A kitchenette, dinette, and a couch that folded out into an additional bed finished it out.

We eventually camped close to two years in two different camping trailers, the second one a thirty-two foot trailer. We did not particularly like the trailers. We felt closed in. I told my husband I felt like a sardine in a tin can. My camping claustrophobia was not due to either of the trailers' floor plans. They were both nice trailers with fairly open floor plans. I just felt closed in.

I felt like I was being shut off from the great outdoors when we were camping right smack dab in the middle of it. At this point, we had gone to the other camping extreme.

Whereas in the tents we did everything out in the open, in the camping trailer, we did everything inside the camper. We were no longer experiencing the nature that was right outside our doorstep. And, since being in the outdoors is part of what camping is to me, I really wanted, and still want, that feeling to be a part of my camping experience.

Photo by Steve Allee

A Chipmunk with his "carry-out" meal.
It is his home, help keep it G.R.E.E.N.

Now we are back in a pop-up with a slide-out dinette. This is our sixth pop-up and it is a 2002 Forest River Flagstaff 425D. We have had this pop-up for several years now. With the tilt out bay window for the sink and stove and the slide out dinette, we have plenty of floor space for the two of us. Occasionally, we take my mother with us and even with the three of us inside we have more than enough room to walk around without bumping into each other.

I know I have already mentioned it, but, my husband appreciates how easy a tent camper is to pull behind our van. He also appreciates the gas mileage that we are able to get pulling a pop-up camper versus a camping trailer.

As we get older, we have discussed getting a motor home and pulling a little car behind us, but my husband is practical and he is a mechanic. His feelings on that are, "Why? I'd just have to work on another motor and keep it running." I guess if we were rolling in dough and could afford to hire someone to do most of the labor on those engines, it would not make any difference. But we do most of our labor on our own.

Need new curtains in the camper? I make them. Tow vehicle motor need an oil change? My husband does it. Need a new bedspread? I get the sewing machine out and make one. Engine got a miss? My husband changes the spark plugs. Want carpet in the camper? We will lay it ourselves. You get the idea. We are do-it-yourselfers. Partly from a certain economic frugal lifestyle and partly due to the fact that most of the time we will do a better job for ourselves then a stranger will anyway. So a motor home is not in our near future.

Maybe someday, when we can afford it, we will purchase a top of the line camping trailer or a fifth wheel with multiple slide outs. But I have to have one with a patio door on one end or the other so I can let all the fresh air inside. Yes, I do like my fresh air when camping. It is my very own secret compulsion.

Yet, with all of my love of camping, I have spent much

of my time camping trying to figure out the best, quickest, easiest, or smartest ways to do things. I searched for books to help me to no avail. I discovered plenty of books for hikers. They take tent camping to a whole other and almost religious level.

I also discovered plenty of books for motor homes and camping trailers. After all, a good number of these owners are retirees with a relatively good income to spend on their RV camping trips. So, of course, there are books out there for them! Consumer marketing will find the money.

However, I have yet to discover even one general all-purpose book strictly for the pop-up camper camping fanatic. Yes, there are a couple of books I found on the mechanics and engineering of the pop-up tent camper, but I do not need those. My husband is so totally qualified on that side of the house, he could write a book himself!

I wanted just a general, have fun, take it easy, relax and enjoy, all purpose book for pop-up campers. We do not make camping a religion, which a hiker or mountaineer will almost have to do to survive. We do not spend the money of an RVer, so many companies are not going to target us as a market. We are just camping for the fun of it and usually on a budget.

We still need ideas, shortcuts, tricks, and tips to make it a good experience. Even an excellent experience. If I had had such a book when we first started camping, I might have spent less time learning how to camp efficiently and more time enjoying camping in the early years.

I have been camping over thirty years now and I like to think I have it down to a fine art. When my husband says we are going camping, I can be packed and ready in thirty minutes. I put our clothes in two suitcases and drinks and perishable food into two coolers and I am ready. Everything else we take with us stays packed and prepared. So I truly hope you can take some of my ideas and adapt them to your camping experience.

Permanent Storage ~ The "Food Box"

In the picture below, you see what I consider to be probably my best-kept top-notch camping secret. This terrific stand-up tool box is packed basically once a season. If any voyeuristic camping enthusiasts could see inside our camper to see how convenient this tool box is to use, everyone would have one! It is in two sections and the top locks onto the bottom. It has wheels and a pull handle which is really convenient. This tool box is my storage cabinet for foods that an RVer would leave in their kitchen cabinets between trips.

Our canvas tool box makes a great permanent "pantry."

I do not like to leave any food in my pop-up. I have never had bugs or ants in my pop-up that were drawn by food stored there and I plan to keep it that way. But there are some foods that are not perishable that I keep packed and ready to go. I store these items in plastic containers with screw-on lids. No pop-off lids are allowed! At the beginning of each camping season, I restock my tool box "pantry" with fresh foods.

My Stocked Food List In My Food Box

_____ Flour, cornmeal, and panko bread crumbs

_____ Bisquick, Jiffy mix, and/or pancake mix

_____ Sugar, brown sugar, and powdered sugar

_____ Sweetener

_____ Salt and pepper

_____ Herbs, spices, and seasonings

_____ Bouillon cubes and/or a can of soup/soup stock

_____ Baking powder and baking soda

_____ Ranch dressing packets and instant soup packets

_____ Coffee and tea bags

_____ Instant hot chocolate

_____ Cider and cinnamon sticks

_____ Kool-aid and lemonade packets

_____ Popcorn (microwave and/or regular), popcorn salt

_____ Pancake syrup, chocolate syrup, and honey

_____ Macaroni and/or rice, maybe instant potatoes

_____ Cold cereal and/or instant oatmeal

_____ Pudding, Jello, cornstarch, tapioca

_____ Worcestershire sauce

_____ Liquid smoke and hot sauce

_____ Two cans of pork 'n beans

_____ One can of green beans (My fave veggie.)

_____ Apple or peach pie filling

_____ Pam or nonstick cooking spray

Variable items:

_____

_____

_____

_____

_____

_____

_____

_____

_____

_____

_____

_____

_____

_____

_____

_____

_____

All of the loose items are stored in air-tight containers. As mentioned previously, I have plastic screw-on lid (not snap-on) containers I store these items in. Before I put the lids on these containers I also lay a piece of plastic wrap over the top. I just feel the plastic wrap adds another layer between the contents and the outside air and keeps my items fresher longer.

I have also had a bad experience with snap-on or press-on lids that came loose and spilled the container's contents all over the bottom of my tub. That created one sweet and sticky, ant-attracting mess that I do not want to ever repeat!

I put the items I will use every trip in the top half of the tool box. These items include coffee, tea, sugar, salt, pepper, etc. Items that I may or may not use, I store in the bottom half. For instance, I may or may not make a dessert using pudding. I may or may not make hot chocolate. We may or may not have cold cereal or oatmeal for breakfast. I may or may not need cornmeal to fry fish. (That, of course, depends on my husband's fishing luck for the day.) My can of green beans is an "emergency" item in case there are no stores near the campground.

By having my "always" items stored in the top half and my "sometimes" items stored in the bottom half, I may or may not even get into the bottom half of my tool box on any given camping trip.

With these items in stock, however, I never have to think ahead of time in too much detail about my menus. I know that whatever I decide to fix, I will have the "fixins" for. And by keeping my tool box stocked with the basics, I know that whatever I would reach for in my kitchen cabinet at home is at hand on our camping trips.

At the end of every camping trip, I restock my tool box immediately upon returning home. That way if we get the chance to go camping again without much notice, my stash is stocked and ready to go. I just wheel it out to the van and load it up. I do not worry about, "Did I restock the coffee? How much sugar is left?"

With the van unpacked and the camper popped up, I just set my tool box on one of my counter tops beside my portable refrigerator and pretend it is my kitchen cabinet. It is a great system. My sister-in-law even adopted this system after she saw me using it a couple of times. She picked her toolbox out at the local discount store. She, also, had been using rubber tubs to pack everything. Don't we all start that way?

My two-piece tool box takes up less space than a plastic tub and I do not constantly have to reach down into the bottom of the tub for the item I am after. With two tiers I do not have everything stacked on top of everything else either. I can wheel the tool box to the van to be loaded, which I could not do with the tub. I had to pick it up and carry the tub everywhere. Not any longer.

All in all, my tool box means my packing time is reduced, my carrying load is reduced, and preparation for my camping trips is a lot less stressful. Since camping should be fun, not stressful, I highly recommend a tool box "cabinet."

Would you look at all those heavy
tubs I used to pack! Not any more!

Cold Storage and Perishables

For cold items, my husband and I finally invested in a couple of those extreme coolers that ice lasts in for days at a time. They are more expensive but I believe they are worth it if you can afford them. We now take just those two five-day extreme coolers with us when camping.

We load the one cooler with iced down beverages and refreshments. (If you have time, put your iced beverages in your refrigerator at home overnight prior to camping. This will help keep your ice frozen longer.) The second cooler is loaded with the perishable food items that I will eventually put in the camper's refrigerator or the portable refrigerator we also carry along on trips. Our portable refrigerator is the same size as our camper's refrigerator. It is one of the luxuries that my husband and I enjoy on longer camping trips.

Once the perishable food cooler is empty, and the pop-up and portable refrigerators are full, we head to the closest store or filling station and fill the coolers with bags of ice. We make sure we keep the coolers in the shade, because even though they are advertised as "extreme" coolers, with a hot sun beating down on them ice still melts at a fast pace. One is usually kept outside under the awning and used as a side table to sit our drinks on.

With clean ice in the previously emptied cooler, we can now go for three, four, even five days without leaving the campground if we do not want to. And since one of my greatest pleasures in camping is to get away from civilization, that makes me one happy camper!

Also, if we can reduce the number of trips we have to make to the store for ice and odds and ends, the time we spend enjoying our camping trip is greatly increased. For a family with children, like my niece and her husband, this two-cooler method definitely increases fun time and decreases the time spent loading up the baby, the baby bag, the toddler, and the teenager, to make a run to the store for ice every day.

The perishable groceries I decide to take will fluctuate with the season and with what I think I will be in the mood to cook. Almost always, though, I will have certain items along. Do modify the following list to suit your family's tastes.

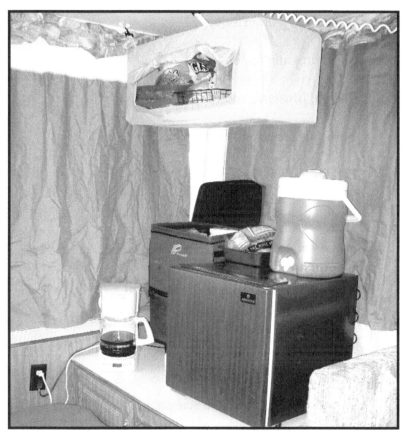

Our "permanent" tool box cabinet with the top open and accessible in the back corner. A portable refrigerator with teeny-tiny freezer, and a favorite "extra," the hanging cabinet. Plus, just for our coffee, three gallons of fresh well water in a jug brought from home.

Perishables Grocery List

_____ Milk and juice

_____ Yogurt and sometimes, pudding cups

_____ Butter, Jelly, and Honey,

_____ Salad dressing and Sour cream

_____ Catsup, Mustard, and Mayonnaise

_____ Barbecue sauce and Steak Sauce

_____ Pickles, relish, salsa

_____ Peanut butter

_____ Eggs

_____ Cooking oil, olive oil, and sesame oil

_____ Potatoes, carrots, and red onions

_____ Corn on the cob (Leave the husks on!)

_____ Whatever vegetable is in season, i.e., asparagus

_____ Tomatoes and lettuce for sandwiches

_____ Apples and bananas

_____ Whatever fruit is in season, (peaches, especially).

_____ Bread, canned biscuits, and buns

_____ Cheese, sliced and a small box of Velveeta

_____ Bacon, ham, and/or sausage

_____ Hamburger (Always!)

_____ Pork chops or steaks

_____ Chicken or venison

_____ Hot dogs and sandwich luncheon meat

Preferred perishables:

_____

_____

_____

_____

_____

_____

_____

_____

_____

Snacks

_____ Jerky

_____ Trail mix

_____ Cookies

_____ Popcorn

_____ Pretzels, Chips and/or Nacho chips

_____ Marshmallows

_____ Chocolate bars

_____ Graham crackers (Got to have s'mores!)

Preferred snacks:

_____

_____

_____

_____

_____

_____

_____

Your grocery list for a camping trip should not be complicated. A good percentage of the food that I take with us on camping trips I simply pull out of my cupboards, the refrigerator, and the freezer. I usually always have potatoes and carrots and items like that on hand, so there is no sense in shopping for new bags of those.

There is almost always some type of meat in my freezer to take, whether we decide we are in the mood for pork chops, venison, or chicken. I do not keep many steaks on hand, though, so we do have to stop at the store for those. But, to make one less trip, we just get them when we are getting ice - providing we go to a regular grocery store and not just a convenience-type mart.

With many of the perishable foods on my list, though, I can either go to the store and purchase them or if I have something on hand, I just drop it in the cooler. For example, we almost always have catsup, mustard, and several condiments on hand. If I have something at home and I do not have to make a store run, I am good to go.

For the items that do not need to be kept cool, I have a picnic basket in which they are packed. The potatoes, of course, go on the bottom with bread and marshmallows on top. Our camper has one of those optional cupboards that hangs from the ceiling and we just place the basket in it after the cupboard is hung. Our snack basket, that I packed for the road trip to the campground, also fits in nice and tidy right inside.

My husband and I really like having that optional hanging cupboard, too. It is very roomy and I am constantly amazed at how convenient that cupboard is! When we first got it, I thought we were just taking advantage of an optional item for the camper that we could afford. It has turned out to be one of my favorite additions to our camper!

We did modify our hanging cupboard so that it hangs where the optional wardrobe is designed to hang. My husband is 6'2" tall. When we first hung the cupboard over the sink where it is designed to hang, he hit his head every time he did anything at the sink or stove. Since I like it when he is cooking or doing dishes, that had to change!

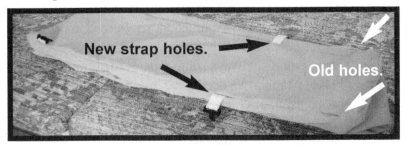

Simple sewing project.

It was a simple sewing project, even for the sewing-challenged like myself. First, measure the distance between the wardrobe hanging hooks on the camper's ceiling. Next, cut two new holes and move the strap in to that point. Then reinforce the area around the new holes with several stitches of strong thread. That is it. With the hanging strap in the new holes, the cupboard is out of the way and very useful.

Personal Packing

Packing our personal items for camping is not all that much different from packing for any trip. There are some things that are with us at all times; our drivers licenses and cell phones for instance. However, I do try to remember to pack my cell phone battery charger. I have forgotten it and for weekend trips, it is no big deal. For a trip of several days, though, I definitely want it with me.

With that in mind, I am not going to list a bunch of things that I think everyone will remember like the check book and credit card. My husband and I usually keep our maps and sunglasses in our van, but if you do not, you will want to remember those as well. Following is my list of things that might not occur to me every time.

Personal Packing List

_____ Cell phone and recharger

_____ Head gear - depending on weather forecast

_____ Cap or visor, bicycle helmet - if bicycling

_____ Jacket and/or sweatshirt

_____ Rain gear and/or umbrella

_____ Swim suits, trunks, and water shoes

_____ Jeans and/or shorts, maybe even bicycle shorts

_____ Tees and tanks

_____ Pajamas and a robe

_____ At least one long-sleeved shirt

_____ Socks and underwear + one extra set for if you get wet.
                           You will want to change to dry.

_____ Belt

_____ Shower shoes and sandals

_____ Hiking boots and tennis shoes

_____ Hair dryer and curling iron

_____ Sunscreen and sunglasses

_____ Insect repellent

Cold weather gear:

_____ Long underwear

_____ Heavy wool "hunting" socks

_____ Gloves and/or mittens

_____ Heavy coat

_____ Winter boots

_____ Hat and earmuffs

Preferred personal items:

_____

_____

_____

_____

_____

_____

_____

_____

_____

Shaving / Shower Kit Content

_____ Prescriptions and/or vitamins

_____ Quarters for the showers that are coin operated

(Keep these in your shower/shaving kit at all times. You will be glad you did when you step into a shower requiring them and you do not have get dressed to walk several hundred yards back to your camper for quarters in the dark! And, yes, I unfortunately speak from experience.)

_____ Sanitizing anti-bacterial hand gel

_____ Soap in soap box, shampoo, and conditioner

_____ Toothbrush, toothpaste, dental floss, mouth wash

_____ Hairbrush, comb, hair holders, and hairspray

_____ Hair dryer and curling iron

_____ Razor and shaving cream

_____ Contact lenses case and solutions

_____ Extra pair of prescription eyeglasses

_____ Deodorant/anti-perspirant

_____ Body lotion, hand lotion, and powder

_____ Foot powder, especially if hiking anywhere

_____ Lip balm and makeup

_____ Toilet paper/kleenex in a waterproof baggie just in case the shower house is out

_____ Tampons or sanitary napkins

_____ Wet wipes

_____ A small flashlight to make the trek back and forth to the shower house in the dark

Unique Needs:

_____

_____

_____

_____

_____

_____

_____

_____

_____

_____

_____

My husband and I each pack one suitcase and one shower kit. There is enough room in our camper's bed to push the suitcases to the back end and still have plenty of room to sleep comfortably. Alternately, sometimes we store them on the opposite bed. We keep our shaving kits packed and ready with travel-sized items at all times. When we get home from a trip, we refill the numerous little plastic bottles when we unpack and we are ready to grab our shower kits and go camping next time.

*Also, take special note and leave the cologne and perfume at home. If you spritz and smell like a flower, a wild berry, or a vanilla treat; trust me, you will attract bees.

My husband checking the tires before
we take off on a weekend trip.
(Yes, we really do use our check lists.)

In The Hamper

If you have not figured it out by now, I really like to be ready to go camping at all times. This means I leave as little as possible to pack at the last minute. Also, I am not too big on packing big plastic tubs that I have to carry around. The tubs themselves weigh a few pounds. Pack them full and you need to be a weight lifter (or my son or husband) to lift them.

We keep our linens and towels ready to go at all times in a cloth hamper that has a zipper top. It is light weight, collapses, and folds away when everything is unpacked. It can also serve as a dirty clothes hamper for the return trip.

No Hamper? Use a Doggie Kennel! If you cannot find a hamper similar to this, go to the pet section of your local discount store. Find the "collapsible" cloth doggie kennels and use one of those. The large size should be plenty big and will work just as well as the round hamper.

Hamper Packing List

_____ Sheets and pillowcases

_____ Bath towels and hand towels

_____ Beach towels

_____ Wash cloths

_____ Dish cloths and towels

_____ Rags for serious accidents

_____ Hot pads, pot holders, and grill glove

_____ Anything washable

Unique Needs:

_____

_____

_____

_____

_____

_____

_____

Again, the minute we get home, I throw these items in the washer. When dry, I fold them and pack them away in the clothes hamper and I am ready to go with clean linens and towels for the next trip. I put new dryer sheets in between some of the folded items and when I pull them out at the campground, my hamper items still smell fresh, even if I packed them a month or two earlier.

(I just saw a laundry hamper with wheels and a pull handle in a catalog! Yes! I see a birthday present in my future.)

A cloth clothes hamper: Much better than a tub!

Under the Dinette Seats

Lightweight items are stored under the seat not located over the trailer's axle.

_____ Coffee pot (wrapped securely in a hand towel).

_____ Battery-powered lantern - If you notice in the below picture, I keep the lantern inside a small trash can. It also has a hand towel wrapped around it to cushion the lantern globe.

_____ Rope lights and citronella candle

_____ Small hand vacuum

_____ Battery charger

_____ Electric burner

_____ Small fan and light combo for hanging over bunks and dinette. These are very nice for reading in bed at night.

_____ A hanging light I made out of a white planter.

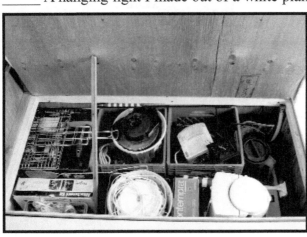

Milk crates work well to keep items neat and tidy.

Heavier items are kept under the seat over the axle. Storing heavier items over the axle helps with weight distribution, pulling ease, and gas mileage.

_____ Our microwave is small, but heavy; therefore, it is stored on the camper's center side of the seat .

_____ A small toaster oven, a vegetable steamer, and slow cooker are also stored here.

_____ We keep our pillows, blankets, mattress pads, and comforters in the camper for the season as these items do not need to be washed after every use. They are used as packing material to cushion our microwave and toaster oven.

_____ Stadium seats to hook over the picnic table benches and to provide a "chair" back to lean against are also stored here.

I highly recommend that anything you store underneath the dinette seats be something that you take out at the beginning of your trip and be done with it. It becomes a nuisance to have to keep pulling the cushions off of the seat to get at something you have stored under them.

Keep a rod inside your seat storage to prop up the seat "lid" when retrieving items.

Recreational List

Depending on what we have planned for our trip, I may or may not need any of these items.

_____ Tickets purchased in advance for any events

_____ Bicycles, spare tubes, and repair kit

_____ Bicycle lock and pump air compressor

_____ Fishing and/or hunting permits

_____ Fishing and/or hunting gear

_____ Backpack, day pack, and/or fanny pack

_____ Water flotation mattress and toys

_____ Water safety jackets

_____ Camera and/or Binoculars

_____ CD player and CDs

_____ Laptop and DVDs

_____ A whistle and compass for emergencies

_____ Walkie talkies and extra batteries

_____ Books, pen and paper

_____ Perhaps even a camping journal

Variable fun items:

_____

_____

_____

_____

_____

_____

_____

_____

Mama Mallard with her ducklings.
It is their home, help keep it G.R.E.E.N.

Prior to the trip, we make sure the camper is ready to go. We carry extra light bulbs and small spare parts in our camper, but if we used something on our last trip, we have to purchase a replacement to be put in the camper on the next trip when we open it up. This is where your pen and paper come in handy. We keep a small tablet out on the table in the camper to make notes for what we will need for our next trip.

We check the air in the tires, the brake lights, and towing lights. A quick walk around and examination of the trailer box itself is also a good idea. There are, however, a few things to make sure that we have or check prior to every trip.

Camper Checklist

_____ Propane tanks filled

_____ Battery charged and charger

_____ Weather radio with fresh batteries

_____ Lantern and flash light with good batteries

_____ Gas, mantles, and funnel if not battery powered

_____ Charcoal and charcoal starter for the grill

_____ The charcoal grill/smoker and/or outdoor camp stove

_____ Fire log or fire wood - local wood only

_____ Fire starter (wax-coated dryer lint works really well)

_____ Matches and/or a lighter

_____ Fire extinguisher

_____ Fire permit, if required

_____ Awning stakes and ropes

_____ Mallet or hatchet and a camp saw

_____ Tire stop chocks for placing behind camper tires

_____ Five gallon water jug filled with fresh drinking water

_____ Water hose and pressure regulator

_____ Heavy duty long electrical cord

_____ Sink waste/grey water collection bucket/tote.

_____ Two very large stainless steel bowls for washing the dishes. Fill these and set them over the coals to get water hot. They must be stainless. You cannot do this with aluminum or rubber dish pans.

_____ Porta potti and biodegradable TP

_____ Lawn chairs and small folding table

_____ Patio mat (not a rug, nor a carpet remnant).

A genuine camping mat lets dirt and water filter through and will not kill any grass if you happen to be on a campsite with grass. They are a little expensive, but worth it as they just sweep clean.

_____ Beach umbrella and stand. Use it to shade the picnic table when not in use at the beach.

Variable camping items:

_____

_____

_____

_____

_____

_____

_____

_____

_____

_____

_____

Most of the Camper Checklist items are kept in the storage bin in the front of our camper. I can easily check the charcoal available for the next trip and once we are set up, with the ends of the camper pulled out, I usually do not need to access that storage area again. There is a side door to use if needed, but this is not true for all camper models.

The porta potti cleaning kit, in particular, is usually stored in an easily accessible spot up front. We can fold everything down at the campsite and be packed, ready to go home, with the porta potti sitting on the hitch to take to the dump site. Then we can access the cleaning kit from outside the camper right at the dump site without the camper being raised. Once the porta potti is clean, we store the cleaning kit and porta potti up in the front storage bin ready for the next trip.

Making Wax-Coated Dryer Lint for a Fire Starter

Slowly melt paraffin/wax block in the top of a double-boiler. You *must* use a double-boiler to do this. When melted to liquid, turn off heat. Next, take the dryer lint and stuff it into the wax, punching it down with a spoon until the wax is completely absorbed. Ladle the mixture into the cups of a cardboard egg carton. Do not use styrofoam. The cardboard will absorb the wax, so make sure you place the carton on something wax-safe. If you do not have a cardboard egg carton, use miniature cupcake cups and place 3-4 in each muffin hole. Let the wax set overnight. When solid, separate the cups and keep in a baggie for the season. To start a fire, just light the corner of the cardboard egg carton cup or the paper muffin cup. Place under your kindling or wood.

Yes, this cottontail rabbit really is pouncing on the red squirrel. All I could figure is it must be a rare mutant ninja attack rabbit.

Inside Cabinet Storage

Every pop-up camper has a few cabinets and drawers for permanent storage. They are not big and there is not a lot of space, so you must make sure that what you pack permanently in your camper is a needed or a very much wanted item.

Our camper has four small drawers, two larger drawers, two small cubby holes, two larger cubby holes, two cabinet areas with doors in addition to the two underneath the sink, and storage underneath both of the dinette seats.

The top drawer holds items we will use the most.

As far as other inside storage is concerned, the top drawer is used to store silverware. I also store matches, lighter, and lighter fluid in this drawer. The second drawer holds our larger grilling utensils, measuring cups, a spatula, and a manual can opener. The third one is my husband's tools and spare parts drawer. The last small drawer holds cards and travel sized board games that we like to play when camping. The two bigger drawers hold candles, serving bowls, aluminum foil, plastic wrap, a miniature cutting board, dishes, bowls, plates, saucers, cups, and plastic drinking glasses.

One of the larger cabinet areas holds our pots and pans. I like to have one very large skillet, a medium skillet, a Dutch oven, and a sauce pan. I keep a miniature muffin tin and cookie sheet inside my toaster oven. With these pots and pans, I can cook virtually anything camping that I can cook at home. My large skillet is Teflon coated and I use it only when I cook inside. My medium skillet, Dutch oven, and sauce pan are cast iron. I put these items right over the fire or in the coals when cooking and it does not hurt them a bit. The food cooked in them is excellent!

The area underneath the sink in our camper is only about six inches deep. We store our dishwashing liquid, cleaning spray, air freshener, Mean Green and other cleaner under the sink. This is also where we store our whisk broom, dust pan, trash bags, baggies, and paper towels (which double as napkins), a small one-gallon bucket to heat water for dishes, some of my spices, and the Pam non-stick spray for pans and for the grill. Clothes pins are kept there also.

One small cubby hole is right next to where our porta potti sits. Naturally we keep our toilet paper there. The other cubby holds the porta potti deodorizing chemicals.

I am careful about what I store in the two larger cubby holes. One of these areas holds the hot water heater with all accompanying tubes and lines and the other

Plates, cups, and plastic wrap, all neat and tidy.

holds the water filter with all accompanying tubes and lines.

In one, under where I place our electric coffee pot, I store coffee filters and a table cloth for the outdoor picnic tables. These are very lightweight items and even if they shift during travel, they will not press against any lines and disconnect them. In the second and slightly larger cubby hole, I keep our cup coolers. Again, these are soft and lightweight items that I know will not disconnect anything during travel.

There is one other area for storage directly underneath the sink that looks like drawers. It has no bottom during travel, but once the sink and stove are raised and set on the cabinet, I can store the dish towels, hot pads, and like items.

Leaving Home for a Few Days

When getting ready for a trip, even after all these years, I will place a pad of paper and a pencil on my kitchen counter. As I think of things that I want to do for a particular trip, I will write them down. As I finish them, I check them off of my list. This is because no matter how many lists I have seen offered in books and on websites (and including my own), I still have to tweak them a little to make them suit my particular trip plan. I am sure you will too.

As far as leaving the house for a few days, I am pretty good about remembering to lock my windows and doors before I leave and I do not usually forget to take care of my pets and farm critters in advance. My husband and I are seldom gone for more than a weekend, but when we are planning a lengthy trip, we have to make plans for the animals and my birds to be fed.

My husband calls our front yard my "feed lot." Okay, so I have six song bird feeders, three finch feeders, six hummingbird feeders, and an Oriole feeder. Add the fact that I feed a feral cat, several red and grey squirrels, an untold number of rabbits, a raccoon and a possum or two, wild turkeys, up to thirteen geese, a few ducks, and eighteen deer (at last count), and I guess there is some truth to his statement. Figure in my indoor cats, my dog, my miniature horse, my miniature mule, and my pygmy goat, and we definitely have a few critters we have to make arrangements for.

Vacation Checklist

_____ Make arrangements for pets, including fresh litter

_____ Contact post office or ask a friend to pick up the mail

_____ Adjust thermostat

_____ Water plants

_____ Unplug computer from electricity and modem

_____ Unplug appliances

_____ Take out trash

_____ Set automatic light timer

_____ Check and lock all windows

_____ Lock all doors, including any garage doors

_____ Pack soft drinks and snacks for the road trip

Vacation checklist extras:

_____

_____

_____

_____

_____

_____

My goal is to make our trip as relaxing as possible. When we are traveling to a campsite, we like to get there before sunset. That way we can scout out the sites and decide which one we like the best. It is also much more pleasant to pop the camper up and set up our site in day light. We can do it at night, but we prefer not to. I am sure the neighbors prefer we not set up in the middle of the night also.

When everything is finally set up, one of the handiest items in our camper is the multiple-tiered hanger that I hang from the camper's pull-down wardrobe in the ceiling. Both my husband's bath towel and wash cloth and mine can hang here to dry as well as a hand towel or two depending on the way I hang the items.

*Remember to snap the pull-down wardrobe rod back up and in place on the ceiling before lowering the roof, otherwise it will break.

Purely for comfort when we were tent camping, my husband and I invested in a couple of self-inflating slim-line mattress pads for sleeping on the ground. For several years they just sat in the back of our closet when we started camping in our pop-ups. Then after one long trip and a week in our pop-up, our mattress seemed to get harder with each passing night. I had an epiphany and upon returning home, I pulled our air mattresses out for our next pop-up camping trip. Those two air mattresses are now permanently stored under the camper mattress. They self-inflate when needed and you simply squish the air out of them and leave them under the mattress for storage when folding down. Our mattress now floats on air. Literally. Yay!

By using the multiple tiered hanger as shown above, I do not need to tie ropes around any trees to use as a clothes line.

Chapter Four
~ Main Entree ~
We Are Here, Now What?

Setting Up Camp

There are as many different ways to set up a camp site as there are different campers and pop-ups. Eventually you will find your favorite way to set up. My husband and I are creatures of habit and pretty much lay out our camp site the same way every time.

If there is a picnic table, our portable charcoal grill goes on the end of that. I see a lot of people placing their portable gas camping stoves in the same spot. If I am going to use gas, I cook inside the pop-up. That is just my preference.

We place our water bucket by the fire pit and whether we use our grill or the fire pit, once we are done cooking a meal, our water goes on the fire to get hot and ready to be used as dishwater. This saves propane use inside the camper.

Our two lawn chairs are under the awning and a cooler in between them. I also have a little folding table that I place right beside the door to the pop-up. I cannot count the number of items that have ended up on that table. It is like our coffee table at home. Whatever I am looking for, if my husband has used it, I guarantee it can be found on that table.

Our patio mat is down and our rope lights are up. They do not attract as many bugs as camping lights and are more ecologically friendly.

We store our bicycles under the front of the pop-up out of the weather and out of the way. The can also be rope-locked to the trailer hitch when they are up front at night. I hang an American flag from a small tent pole that I carry with us and our campsite is complete.

I have seen campsites that seemed to have an entire kitchen out on the table and I have seen camp sites that had absolutely nothing outside. I have seen camp sites that had a small tent that was essentially the play tent. Every toy imaginable was inside that tent. I have seen camp sites with boats and every water toy imaginable parked there. Like I said, camp sites are totally personal. There is no one correct way to do it. You will find what works best for you.

Games and Entertainment

If you have not already figured it out, one of my favorite things to do when camping is purely and totally, absolutely nothing! There is a fine art to relaxation that few of us in today's world have perfected. I claim to be one of those skilled few. When I go camping, I want to sleep, eat, and be lazy. That is all. I do not want to listen to music blasting away. I do not want to watch a movie on the laptop. I do not want to do anything that requires action of any type. And I particularly do not want to listen to the noise of civilization in the form of a radio, TV, CD, cassette tape, cell phone, or anything else.

An entire drawer full of games for times of inclement weather.

However, on occasion, my husband likes a diversion or two. If I am lucky, I can send him fishing or we go boating. If we are not boating, we usually take our bicycles with us when we camp, so we will take a nice bike ride.

Bike Riding: Riding your bicycles up to the shower house is not only a good morning exercise, it saves gas. It is also a fun way to covertly spy out and compare the neighbor's camping gear and pop-up. Oh, yes, you will learn, this is essential when camping. It is voyeurism at its best! I once saw a tiny solar panel that one camper was using to light his pop-up with as he was in a campsite with no electricity! How innovative! That is taking low impact camping to new heights of awareness!

Day Hikes: When we are not bike riding, there is always the option of walking around the camp grounds. Or, if there are trails, my husband and I will sometimes go on a day hike. If you decide to hike as a recreational activity, be sure you stay on the trails, take plenty of water along, and wear good hiking boots. If it is a well-traveled trail, you might be able to get away with tennis shoes. But, you need to know in advance the type of trail you will encounter a mile or two in.

Keep in mind here that I am not writing a "hiking" book or talking about "back packing" into a remote area. I am talking about taking light hikes that are well-traveled and actually a part of the camp ground. I call it "casual hiking" or a "day hike."

Most dogs swim adequately. However, if you are going boating, your dog needs a life vest, too.

Day Hike Checklist

_____ Water, juice, and/or electrolyte drink

_____ Small pack/ruck   _____ Snack and/or lunch

_____ Camera/Binoculars   _____ Small First Aid Kit

_____ Lighter or *dry* matches   _____ Swiss Army knife

_____ A whistle - (The next time I get lost, I can whistle
                          loudly and not lose my voice hollering.)

Personal Hiking Choices:

_____

_____

_____

_____

Persimmons are not ripe until after the first hard frost.

Gathering: One fun thing my husband and I like to do is to identify the trees around us. We have had several pleasant snacks from a few of those trees we have spotted. We have eaten pecans and made fresh pecan pie. We have eaten paw-paws before the deer got them all -

which is quite a feat! The paw-paw tree looks kind of like a palm tree and the fruit is shaped like a short, stubby purple banana.

Wild Blackberries

I have made a persimmon chutney from that tasty fruit. Granted, you really have to know your trees - because I am not recommending you pop anything into your mouth that you do not know with absolute certainty what it is! That is not smart and it could even be deadly. Do not do it! But, my husband and I do recognize a few wild edibles and we sometimes like to take advantage of the "fruit of the hunt," so to speak.

Wild blackberries are usually easy to find, but beware! Those bushes do not give up their bounty easily and they have plenty of thorns to prick you and give you a few bloody pricks and scratches.

One of my favorite wild fruits without thorns to battle is the mulberry which grows on a tree. Always wash your fruits well when picking them wild. Chances are they will have a few small insects hiding in their crevices, especially mulberries.

One of my favorite trees: The Mulberry

If you know the area you are staying in well, and it is the first

Morel Mushrooms

warm spell in the Spring think about hunting for some Morel mushrooms. I do not believe there is a better meal on the planet than freshly caught fish and fried morel mushrooms.

Morels are very distinctive with their pits and ridges. They look like a little honeycomb on a stem. And, important to note, the bottom edge of the morel's cap is attached to the stem.

Do not confuse true Morels with the False Morel. The false morel can make your violently ill and can even cause death. False morels have lobes, folds, wrinkles and flaps, but no pits or ridges like a true morel. Also, the bottom edge of the cap hangs free around the stem, like a skirt.

If you are not sure what mushroom you are picking to eat, it is best to just leave it in the forest. For years I have been told about the "beef steak" mushroom that grows here in Missouri and how good this mushroom is to eat. People have waxed eloquent about it to me. However, I do not know what it looks like! I have seen several mushrooms I suspect were this edible mushroom but I am not absolutely certain. Needless to say, those mushrooms were never harvested by me.

See *The Audubon Society Field Guide to North American Mushrooms* for more information.

If I am not one hundred percent positive what I am picking, I do not eat it. This goes for mushrooms, fruit, nuts, and greens. Yes, almost every Spring I can be found gathering "greens." This is a tradition that has been passed down in my family for generations and I can be seen along roadsides proudly gathering my "dock" and "lambs quarter." Boil these greens like spinach, add some bacon or ham hocks, and you have a yummy old-fashioned Ozark Hills meal.

Star Gazing: Take a star chart with you when you camp. Street lights and business lights in towns and cities light up the night sky and the stars do not seem very bright. Get away from those lights and sit out under the stars in a State Park or U.S. Army Corps of Engineers Park where there are no street lights and you will be amazed at how bright the stars in the night sky can be.

Which constellations you identify will depend on the time of the year you are stargazing, the time of the night, and where you are camping. Most of us are familiar with the Big Dipper, the Little Dipper, and the North Star. There are 88 constellations in the night sky to discover. The major ones we can spot here in North America are Ursa Major, Ursa Minor, Cassiopeia, Cehpeus, and Draco.

If you do not want to rack your brain trying to find the constellations, make up your own. It is cloud watching at night. Remember when you were a child and you spotted a rabbit in the clouds? Chances are you can find one in the stars at night. On a clear night, if you are lucky you might spot a shooting star. Remember to make a wish! And, did you know that you can also see five different planets with the naked eye at night? Take some time to find them. They are Mercury, Mars, Venus, Saturn, and Jupiter.

Bird Watching: Whether I am at home, hiking, fishing, hunting, or camping, one of my favorite things to do is bird watch. If you think you are not a birdwatcher, you might try it. I, myself, am a couch potato bird watcher. If it lands within eyesight, I am good. I am not so avid a bird watcher that I actually go looking for them. However, do not write me off just yet.

While I have been camping, just here in Missouri, I have seen a lot of beautiful birds that I would never have seen in town. Two of the brightest colored are the Red-headed and Pileated Woodpeckers. I cannot even begin to describe the deep, beautiful color of their heads.

My favorite bird is probably the Indigo Bunting. The male Indigo Bunting is a deep sapphire, almost cobalt, blue. My husband and I first saw the Indigo Bunting when we rode the Katy Trail. Since then, I have managed to attract them to my back yard. I feel so fortunate to have this bird at my bird feeders.

Another bird we first saw when camping was a shore bird, the Killdeer. Unlike most people who say, "Spring is here," when they see the first Robin, my husband and I say, "Spring is here," when we first hear a Killdeer. They have a distinctive call very easy to recognize. Stan Tekiela has written several *Field Guides*, which have excellent photos with which to easily identify birds, trees, wildflowers, or mushrooms.

Other birds we have seen camping are Canadian geese, Mallards, Hummingbirds, Downy woodpeckers, Bluebirds, Orchard Orioles, Wild Turkey, and Scarlet Tanagers. Now there is a bird that stands out in a crowd. The male Scarlet

This Sparrow has just captured a moth lunch for the day.

Tanager is as boldly fire-engine red as the Indigo is cobalt.

There is a method and discipline to be followed to enjoy nature. In order to see these birds, or any other wildlife, you cannot be sitting in your campsite with the music blaring or the dog barking. (You can do that at home anyway.) Feel nature inside you. It *can* be felt, but you have to be quiet and let nature tip-toe peacefully into your soul. Then while you are relaxing, you will spot a ruby or a sapphire in a tree. Move slowly and look closely, and you will be rewarded with a glimpse of one of God's jewels of nature.

My husband and I have watched deer move within ten feet of our campsite by being still. We have also been visited by ground squirrels a time or two. Those little guys are hilarious to watch. And we almost always see a rabbit or two.

Games: When we are not communing with nature, sometimes we play cards or a game. We have one of those board games that I keep in the camper that has multiple games you can play. We also store a Frisbee for those times when we want to do something a little more active. It is flat, light-weight, and takes up practically no space.

This is the only time I have ever seen a bird on top of another. I do not know if Killdeer do this a lot or not.

Ladder Golf

One game that you will see a lot of when camping is Ladder Golf. Two bolo-style golf balls are tossed toward a rack of three tiers. Scores are determined by which tier they wrap around. This is a great game to play and easy to pack. It takes a lot more skill to play than expected and young and old alike can play. Just be careful that young children do not use the bolo golf balls as flying missiles!

Another game that is fun when you are off camping is Hillbilly Horseshoes. You might know it as Washer Toss. Regardless of the name used, the basic premise is to toss large washers as you would in the game of Horseshoes. You can lay different size rings on the ground or sometimes you will see enterprising wooden boxes with different sizes of PVC pipe inside to toss the washers at. The elite ones are carpeted to

Hillbilly Horseshoes

muffle the sound of the washers. It is a fun game that all ages can play. If you do not have washers to toss, use bean bags.

The key to enjoying your time camping is to find something you like to do and just hang out. I love to read. My husband - not so much. So if he does choose to go fishing, I usually take a book and bury my nose in the book. We are together, both doing something we like to do. We do not have to have conversation. We just relax together.

And do not be shy of your neighbor. One of the best times my husband and I ever had camping was when a neighbor came over and asked us if we would be on their softball team. As the gentleman explained, it was going to be the adults against the children. So far he had four adults and about twelve children. He desperately needed our help. My husband and I looked at each other, shrugged, and said, "Sure," and off we went to play ball.

I do not remember any of the names of any of the people we played with, but I do remember how much fun we had! So if you are getting a game going, ask the neighbors to join in. You might make a new friend, or you might just make a fond memory, like I did. Either way, the experience is sure to be worth it.

Occupying Children: Leave the video games and the computers at home. Try playing Nature's Tic-Tac-Toe. Make a Tic-Tac-Toe sheet with different plants and/or animals in the squares. Make the center square Poison Ivy and teach kids to recognize it and avoid it at all costs! The first child to find or spot a straight line wins! Or make it Nature's Bingo. "B" is for birds. "I" is for insects. "N" is for nature (all other animals). "G" is for anything green (grass, trees, and flowers). "O" is optional (clouds, fish, etc.).

Give your children something to do when camping. Take along a small microscope or a telescope. At the very least, get them a pair of binoculars or a magnifying glass. Help them draw a picture of their discoveries for identification and further research when they are at home on their computer.

Keep your eyes open. You never know just what Mother Nature might decide to show you. The emergence of this "Katydid" took over two hours.

For instance, I learned a lot of things just writing this book. I never knew bugs were so tasty! When I researched the cicada, I found out that, like grasshoppers and locusts, they are edible! Deep fry or barbecue and grill them, preferably the soft ones that have just emerged, and eat them with some cocktail sauce, as you would a crawdad (pictured on page 109). However, you normally boil the crawdads. Of course, if you have shellfish allergies, you do not want to eat any of them. And, there is a possible risk of pesticide poisoning when eating cicadas and other bugs, so choose your harvesting area with care. Okay, I admit it, I added that with tongue in cheek - and that is where it is staying. Although it is true they are edible, I am not eating

Finally, totally emerged, this cicada immediately started climbing up the tree.

any! But, I will eat frog legs as long as I do not have to cook them. Yes, they do jump around in the pan.

Challenge your child to identify animal scat and animal tracks. There are kits available to make plaster casts of the animal tracks. Teach them the difference in mammals, marsupials, reptiles, etc. Or, research an animal before your trip and prepare questions for your child to answer. Pick a different animal each trip.

Your child might find it fascinating to learn about the humble Opossum. The 'possum is North America's only marsupial. Meaning, it is an animal with a pouch, like kangaroos. Females carry up to fourteen babies in their pouch. Opossums have opposable thumbs on their hind feet. The opossum is also the only North American mammal with a prehensile tail. Prehensile tails have the ability to "grasp" onto things, like limbs, to help them climb.

Do opossums really hang by their tails? Do they "play dead" when they feel threatened? Do opossums curl up, lay flat, or both? Do they release a repulsive smelling fluid that smells like rotting meat when playing dead? If you pick just one animal to research with your child, it would be hard to top the shy and nocturnal Opossum.

July through October is "Froggin' Season" in Missouri and a permit is required to harvest frogs.

Above: Goose tracks. See the web outline?

Below: An Opossum's rear foot track.

Do NOT Transport Non-Native Species

Not only it is *not* ecologically responsible to transport fire wood or fish bait from one area to another, it is also not responsible to transport insects from one area to another. A bug found in one part of the country that is transported to another part of the country and let loose, can and frequently does, disrupt the local ecosystem as a feral newcomer. Conservation departments even have a term for these invaders: They are called "invasive species" and can refer to plants, animals, insects, fungi, and any other organism introduced to an area outside their native habitat.

When any non-native or alien "species" are introduced to an area, if there is not a natural predator in that same area, the "alien species" can become the new "swamp monster," even when introduced for good reason.

Take for example the state of Missouri's introduction and purposeful planting of the Asian plant, sericea lespedeza, along roadsides to prevent erosion. This plant has no predators in Missouri. None of our cattle, deer, or equine species feed on it and it has now spread aggressively and is disrupting native plants. My own hay fields are now infested with the junk and not even my goat will eat it! Non-native species are not good.

Crawdads can be substituted for lobster in almost any recipe.

A crawdad / crayfish, a relative to the lobster, with eggs underneath her tail. (See the arrow.)

Bugs, Bites, Stings, and First Aid

I can hear it now. Readers are saying to themselves, "Why did she put Bugs with Bites and First Aid?" Ever heard of Lyme Disease? That is why. It seemed logical at the time.

I do not like some bugs. I am perfectly aware that they have a place in the universe. I just do not want them interfering with my camping "universe." Mosquitoes, flies, fleas, and ticks, at the very least, carry germs from one spot to another and they can carry disease. Bee and wasp stings can be fatal. I just do not want to attract them and I want to repel them to the best of my ability! I guess I am just unreasonable that way. Let me start with the most annoying irritant.

Repelling Mosquitoes

When camping, I use citronella candles to keep Mosquitoes at bay. They work tolerably well and if there is a particularly annoying swarm of them, I can also light a mosquito coil. Between these two preventative measures my camping trips have almost always been mosquito tolerable, and generally mosquito free, I am happy to say.

I did have one adventure with mosquitoes that I hope I never repeat, though! When my husband and I were on the Katy Trail bike camping trip, we had stopped to take a picture of some deer we spotted down in a bog on the side of the trail. It was a doe and her fawn, and they both looked so gentle and

The Preying Mantid or Praying Mantis is an interesting bug often confused with a Walking Stick.

beautiful. God had certainly graced us with an award-winning photograph opportunity. The sun was warmly shining through the tree leaves. Golden light dappled the mirror calm water. The deer were so peaceful and ... whoa doggies! *I have never been swarmed so fast and bombarded so furiously in my entire life. Get me out of here!*

The minute my husband and I stopped our bikes and I turned to retrieve the camera from the bike bag, there were thousands, and I do mean hundreds of thousands, of mosquitoes swarming us. When we waved our arms through the air to disperse them, we literally felt them brushing against our arms they were so thick. I have never felt the like!

I never did get a picture of those deer. We scrambled to get back on our bikes and get the ... blankety blank ... out of dodge! Take note: We had insect repellent on, not just Avon's Skin So Soft, like usual, but actual chemical insect repellent! We have decided that if we ever do the Katy Trail again, not only will we wear insect repellent through that particular stretch, it will be the heavy duty kind!

But, back to bugs and camping. Another easy way to keep mosquitoes at bay is to take along a box fan and set it up outside where you have your lawn chairs or camping chairs. Sounds goofy, I know. A fan outside? But it really works. Mosquitoes do not stick around where there is a good breeze blowing and if you are camping in the heat of summer, the fan feels good.

I do not use a lot of unnatural chemicals when I am camping. Skin So Soft and Citronella are about as chemical-minded as I get. Avon's Skin So Soft repels Mosquitoes on me while it is softening my skin and Citronella repels them in my air space. That works for me.

Another prettier way to deter Mosquitoes is to take along a little pot of marigolds, basil, and lemon grass to set on your picnic table. If you are going to be somewhere for more than just a weekend, this works really well. You have a pretty center piece on your table, and flying insects really do not like the smell of marigolds. By the way, my "pot" is sometimes a mop bucket. The bucket handle makes it very easy to pick it up off the front porch, put it in the back of the tow vehicle, and then carry it to the picnic table at the campsite. I do not have to pick it up with both hands like I would an actual flower pot. Basil also repels cockroaches.

An added plus is that lemon grass is the plant that citronella oil is harvested from. If pesky Mosquitoes or gnats are hovering, break off a piece of lemon grass and rub it between your hands to release the oils. Then just rub your hands over your arms and neck or whatever skin is exposed. Voila! You have made a natural mosquito and gnat repellent. There is also a plant called the "citronella" plant that is leafy like a marigold that works well to repel Mosquitoes.

Burning sage also repels Mosquitoes. I just sprinkle it over my mosquito coil. Do not sprinkle too much, you will put the coil out. By doing this I have a continuous smoking effect of the sage while the coil burns down. Between the bucket, the citronella candle, the coil, and the sage, Mosquitoes take to the hills! Plus, I like the smell of the smoking sage.

Small Box Turtle with a built-on camper shell.

Missouri is home to seventeen kinds of turtles and both the smallest and the largest fresh water turtles in the world. All but three are protected. Check *Missouri's Wildlife Code* for season and limit on the three game turtles.

Repelling Chiggers

Now that you know how to repel the irritating flying pests, what about the sneaky ones? I am talkin' chiggers! I swear, I do not know how one teeny, tiny critter can cause so much itching and scratching! Fortunately, while I was in the Army I had an experienced non-commissioned officer tell me how to keep from getting chiggers when I was on a road march or bivouac.

He told me to use powdered sulfur. It works! All you do is sprinkle powdered sulfur in your sock, maybe a teaspoon amount, and then smush it around so that your entire sock is "powdered." Put your socks and shoes on and go about your business. The powder consistency of the sulfur also helps keep sweat to a minimum on the ole tootsies. I love powdered sulfur! You can find it at your local pharmacy.

You may have heard that you can get a couple of flea collars and wrap them around your ankles. I know I have had sweet grandmotherly gardeners tell me they do this when they are out gardening. This is not recommended. Flea collars can be toxic to some people.

Shoo, Fly, Shoo

My husband abhors the common house fly. When we are camping he will cut down the fly population. If he is sitting outside, he has a fly swatter in hand. The fan circulating the air helps keep flies away, but sometimes it is not enough.

So that hubby does not spend his entire weekend hunting flies, my marigold and lemon grass bucket also contains lavender, basil, and mint. I can use the mint for tea, the basil for cooking and flies do not like either the mint or the lavender. If the flies seem to be ignoring my repellent, I simply reach over and crush a leaf or two of mint or marigold. This releases the odor into the air and the flies leave.

On a side note and totally off the subject of repelling insects: Scorpion flies fascinate me. You will probably never be aggravated by this shy, solitary fly, but I just had to include it in the book. It is a beautiful fly! When the male goes courting, he displays his orange and black wings and he moves his body enticingly (he hopes) as he secretes his scent. In addition, he takes a gift to the female, usually a dead insect or a house fly. If she likes the gift, she will offer herself and then eat the insect during copulation. The bigger the gift, the longer the copulation. Other than celebrating their nuptials, Scorpion flies feed mainly on nectar and pollen, thereby helping honeybees pollinate crops. *As the numbers of both of these beneficial insects are decreasing, please do not kill this particular fly, the Scorpion Fly or our Honeybees.*

Even though his tail looks wicked, the Scorpion Fly neither stings nor bites humans.

Repelling Ants

Having gotten this far in my book, you know that I have had gooey messes in the bottom of my plastic tubs that could have attracted ants in my early days of camping. I was spared the ants in my camper, but I have had them in the kitchen at home. How do they find a way in? And what attracted them? I have no idea.

I managed to get rid of them by spraying Mean Green on their trail. Not only did it kill them instantly, but the cleaning detergent apparently wiped out their scent trail. Mean Green is a chemical, but, it is safe enough to use with my bare hands to clean with. In my estimation, that makes it a much better ant deterrent than any ant killer spray that I would still have to clean up after I have sprayed it in order to prevent my cats from stepping in it and licking it off of their paws.

If you have had ants coming in your pop-up, spray your wheels, trailer tongue, and anything in contact with the ground with Mean Green. They will not come back. When I pull into a new campsite, one of the first things I do is clean the picnic table with Mean Green and spray around the table legs and camper tires. This usually keeps the ants off the table for the duration of our stay and out of our camper also. Sometimes if we are staying for more than a day or two, I reapply. Mean Green works!

Other people have told me they have used pepper, cayenne pepper, and pepper oils to deter ants. I personally have not tried these methods, but I have no reason to doubt those who passed this wisdom on.

Repelling Fleas

That covers what I consider the most intrusive pests to humans when camping. But what about my pooch? Fleas just love him. And there is not enough love in the world for me to embrace him when he is being invaded by fleas. Sorry, Pup.

Fortunately, I know that fleas not only do not like lemons or citrus smells, but lemon water will actually kill a flea. Cut a lemon or two in half, pour boiling water over the halves (skin and all), and let cool. Squeeze all the lemon juice out of the lemon and lemon oils out of the skin that you can. Take a sponge and rub onto your pooch. It kills fleas instantly and your doggie smells lemony fresh.

To help keep fleas from coming back and reinstating themselves on your pooch, carry a pillow case with you that you can put cedar shavings into and make that pillow case your dog's bed sheet. The cedar oils repel fleas and are also a wonderful doggie area freshener.

Repelling Ticks

There is one more critter that I do not like to mess with when camping. Where I live, however, I might as well face it. Just about once a day I am going to find one crawling on me come Spring time and then I feel like I have a dozen crawling on me. I hate them! I am talking about a relative of chiggers: Ticks. Ugh. Ick. Blecch. Talk about a nasty critter.

Not only are they just a plain nasty dirty blood-sucking critter, they can carry Lyme disease, Rocky Mountain disease and several others serious diseases. If you are going to be somewhere that ticks are prevalent, use insect repellent and do not mess around! Prevention and avoidance are best when it comes to these nasty buggers.

If you find one on you and it is not imbedded, pick it off of your skin and kill it. If it is imbedded, you need to take an extra precaution when removing it so that you do not leave its head or pinchers in your skin.

A tick's mouth parts have reverse harpoon-like barbs, designed to penetrate and attach to skin. They also secrete a cement-like substance that helps them adhere firmly to the host like super glue. Lovely.

So how do you remove these parasites? Do not use tweezers! Yeah, I know. Most first aid books, medical professionals, and even the Lyme Disease website says to use tweezers. But, squeezing the tick will only encourage it to move deeper into your skin. Not only that, squeezing the tick, breaking off the mouth parts, or rupturing the tick's body can allow fluids to escape that may contain disease and bacteria.

Why risk that when there are really, really, simple tick removal products on the market that work? Get an actual tick remover and slowly, very slowly, pull up on the tick. A tick remover is no larger than your thumb and is just a piece of flat metal that has a "V" shaped area at the end. They can easily be carried in your wallet all year long. You scoop the metal under

Pro-Tick Remedy

the tick and wedge his head in the center of the V. Then you just lightly and firmly start lifting up. Be patient. Very patient! That tick is not going to let go easily. It can take a good 30 to 60 seconds to get the tick to voluntarily let loose. It is a long few seconds, too. When all you are doing is looking at a tick waiting for it to back itself out of your skin, you might want to rush things. You might be tempted to go grab the tweezers and just yank! Do not do it. Slow and easy is the only way to go with this one. Do not twist and turn the tool, do not tug too hard. You want the tick to voluntarily pull itself out of your skin, body, pinchers, head and all! And it will. Eventually. In a minute or so.

Once you have the tick removed safely from your skin, keep it. Put it in a baggy or a jar. If the spot around the bite turns reddish with a pale center and you begin to have muscular pain, headaches, and fever, go see your doctor. Like now! You may have Lyme disease. It can affect the nervous system, your joints, and even your heart. By keeping the tick, your doctor may be able to identify Lyme disease quicker.

If you do not have a tick remover, cover the tick with vaseline or liquid soap and cut off its air supply. This is said to cause the tick to release its hold so it can be removed. That is what they told me in the Army. I have tried this and it does work to a certain extent. Once the tick is smothered, it does seem to release easier. On the other hand it also seems to kill them and sometimes they do not back out. I guess you just have to be patient tugging on them with a bona fide tick removal tool. Do take time with this. Either way, after you have handled a tick, wash your hands! Not only may their fluids cause Lyme Disease and Rocky Mountain Spotted Fever, they are just nasty.

Immediate Treatment of Bites

Previously I ended with what I consider to be one of the nastiest bugs on the planet and how to repel them or remove them. Now I am going to start with how to treat the bites of that same critter and the others. Up front, though, I have recently found a new favorite treatment for all itching, whether from a bite or a poison ivy rash. The remedy is the liquid from the stem of the Jewel Weed plant. This works in approximately 95% of the population. (See Poison Ivy.)

Tick Bites

The obvious first step is to wash the area with warm, soapy water and rinse. I seem to be allergic to tick bites even without them carrying Lyme, or any other type, disease. So for a tick bite, I will also use hydrogen peroxide. That is just what I do. After I am sure the bite is as disinfected as I can get it, I will then put an anti-bacterial cream on it with hydrocortisone in it to relieve the itch and pain.

Let me repeat, if the spot around the bite turns reddish with a pale center go see your doctor. Or, if you begin to have muscular pain, headaches, neck or back pain, and fever, go see you doctor. Lyme disease may or may not be preceded by a lesion. As many as 25% of tick bites carrying Lyme's may or may not results in lesions.

Be aware, also, your symptoms may not appear until a month after infection. If these symptoms are ignored or attributed to something else, the second stage of the disease could include heart palpitations, chest pain, difficulty in breathing or shortness of breath, brief periods of loss of consciousness, general malaise, large joint arthritis, or neuropathy.

The alarming symptoms above will send almost anyone to a doctor; just remember to tell him or her about your tick bite! The third phase of Lyme's disease may include recurring bouts of arthritic pain, chronic fatigue, general malaise, mood changes, insomnia, and memory loss.

Mosquito Bites

For Mosquitoes, rub some camphor phynique on the bite. This stuff stinks to high heaven, but it is what Grandmas through the years always used and it still seems to work best on mosquito bites. There are also several products on the market advertising "anti-itch" capability. Jewel Weed works too. You might wonder why I keep mentioning Jewel Weed. It is a simple, no-cost solution that works. I am lucky to have almost a half acre growing on my farm, but it grows in many wooded areas around camp grounds. (See Poison Ivy.)

Chigger Bites

Chiggers burrow into your skin cells around very thin skinned areas, such as the ankles, behind the knees, and the crotch area. They are so tiny that contrary to popular belief, they do not even make it truly into your skin proper, just into the outer layer of cells. Either way, they itch!

By the time you start itching, most chiggers are already gone and they have just left their saliva behind. This saliva contains digestive enzymes that are literally dissolving the skins cells it comes in contact with so the chigger could dine on the liquefied cells. The human body is a miraculous machine, though, and it immediately started hardening the cells around the bite to prevent more liquefication. And, wallah! The chigger now has a human straw, called a stylostome, from which to suck your liquefied cells. Eeeewh.

Since it is actually the body's self-protecting stylostome that is irritated and itches, take heart. The chigger is gone. They are so tiny that even the slightest touch will knock them off. Eventually, in a week to ten days, your body will absorb the stylostome and heal it like any other "scab." Until that time, to relieve itching, first try hydrocortisone cream, Caladryl, or camphor. Or try Jewel Weed.

If the bites are still itching, I personally resort to desperate measures. I will get my fingernail polish out (I always carry clear for just this purpose), and I will dab the polish on the bites. Aaaah. Instant relief. The bite does not go away, but the itching is relieved.

Be aware, though, this is not a perfect remedy. After a day or two the polish will start itching and maybe even causing an irritated red spot. Remove the polish with polish remover. Rub the hydrocortisone cream on the spot and all will again be well. Because by this time, the body has performed considerable healing on the stylostome.

Bee, Wasp, and Velvet Ant Stings

Have you ever heard of a "cow killer" ant? Here in Missouri they are relatively common and one species or another exists in all lower 48 states. But they are not an ant at all. They are a wasp. The female has no wings and is commonly mistaken for an ant. A huge, gigantic, beautiful, velvety, rust-red ant, I feel obligated to add.

We have these ant-look-alike wasps on our farm and you could not pay me to touch one. They did not get the nick name "cow killer" for nothing. I figure with a nick name like that, their sting must pack a wallop. And, no, their venom is not really strong enough to kill a cow. Like any other bee or wasp, their sting is not normally venomous enough to kill a person either, unless they have an allergy to bee or wasp venom.

Velvet Ant

119

I mention this wingless beauty, pictured at 100% actual size on the previous page, because if you are camping with someone who is allergic to bee stings, I want you to recognize that this particular wasp may not have wings. Therefore, it may not be recognized as a "bee" sting. If you are deathly allergic to wasp stings, do not ever be without your anti-histamine and medication. Make sure the people you are camping with know where it is also and how to use it!

If the bee has left their stinger in your skin, just scrape it out with the edge of a knife. Again, do *not* use tweezers to accomplish this. You may squeeze more venom into the skin.

Cicada Killer

For those of us who are not allergic to bee stings, they are still extremely painful! Take some baking soda and ice cold water (out of the bottom of the cooler is best) and make a paste. Plaster this paste onto the area stung. This is a very soothing paste.

Remember, while we are used to thinking of being stung by a "flying" wasp or bee, a lot of these insects, including the huge black and yellow Cicada Killer wasp, pictured above, make their nest in the ground. Keep your eyes open for their nests when walking.

Scorpion Stings

I always thought scorpions existed just in deserts. That is, until I opened my mother's lake cabin up one Spring day and spotted a scorpion on the back porch. I thought I was seeing things. I hollered for witnesses to be sure I was really seeing a scorpion! Having missed a prime opportunity to photograph a scorpion in Missouri, I headed to the internet to discover, that yes, about ninety species of scorpions exist all over the United States. Even in a moist area like a wooded lake lot, there may be scorpions. Well that made my day. Not.

All but four of the scorpion species naturally occur West of the Mississippi River and happily, at least for me, the only deadly scorpion native to the United States is found in Arizona. That still left me with my buddy here in Missouri, the Striped Scorpion, normally not considered dangerous to humans. Scorpion stings, regardless of geographic location should be treated as potentially dangerous unless the scorpion can be positively identified. Like bee stings, if a person is allergic to the sting, the consequences can be deadly.

Wash the bitten area with soap and water. Apply a cool compress and elevate the area. If difficulty in breathing, blurred vision, muscle twitching, a "thick tongue" sensation, or roving eye movements and hyperactivity develops (especially in children), seek medical attention.

Spider Bites

The critters just keep getting creepier and leggier. Now, I think their webs are beautiful pieces of art when there is dew sparkling on them, and while researching arachnids for this book, I came to appreciate them more than I expected. I was surprised to learn that approximately 80% of suspected spider bites in the U.S.A. are actually caused by other insects, such as ticks.

Cocooning food for liquefication and consumption later.

121

All spiders have some amount of venom with different degrees of potency. The venom is used to immobilize and preserve their prey before storing it in a cocoon for dining on later.

Spiders do not "eat" anything. They actually have filters to drain out solid food. They "drink" their food. To do so, they will inject digestive enzymes into their prey to decompose it right inside its own shell, and then slurp it up.

Fortunately for humans, most spider's fangs, are either too short or too fragile to penetrate the skin. Besides that, most spiders do not even want to confront humans. They would rather go the other way. Good for them, I say!

However, spider bites are painful and in some instances deadly. Spider bites are almost always too small to be seen easily. You probably will not even know you have been bitten until redness, itching, and swelling occurs later. A spider only bites once, leaving two tiny fang holes. If there are multiple bites present, fleas or chiggers are probably the culprits.

The Black Widow: The most dangerous spider in the United States is the Black Widow spider. The venom of the Black Widow is twelve times more potent than that of a Rrattlesnake. (It is a good thing this spider is not the size of a Tarantula!) There are six different species, such as the Brown Widow spider in Louisiana, and they are all mostly found in the southern United States. The Black Widow is a shiny, black spider, with a large round belly that has a red or orangish-red "hourglass" on the underside. This one's bite is considered "medically significant" to humans. While it can be deadly, with modern medicine there has not been a death attributed to a Black Widow in the United States for almost a decade.

Black Widow bite symptoms include muscle pain in the abdomen, back, and limbs, as well as other parts of the body, hypertension, nausea, and sweating. If you suspect you have been bitten by a Black Widow, seek medical attention.

The Brown Recluse: This brown spider, with the violin shape on its back, while not as deadly poisonous as previously thought, still commands some serious respect. People across the United States erroneously think the Brown Recluse exists everywhere. Not so. The Brown Recluse is mainly found from East Texas up to Kansas, east toward mid-Tennessee and south to Alabama. Other Recluse species are not even as venomous as the Brown Recluse.

According to studies reported in the *Journal of Medical Entomology*, the Brown Recluse is not considered deadly at all and is in fact more likely to run and hide than attack. It comes by the name "Recluse" honestly. And, apparently there is not one proven Brown Recluse death anywhere in the United States. It is now believed by some entomologists that the Brown Recluse has been wrongfully accused in cases that were actually Lyme Disease or Hobo Spider bites.

Almost every report ever printed or quoted reads that the Brown Recluse is deadly poisonous - and now it seems that simply is not true. In some areas, physicians have reported more bites by the Brown Recluse than the number of verified Brown Recluse spiders, *Loxosceles reclusa,* spotted or collected in the same area - in over one hundred years of recorded arachnological data! Talk about a huge discrepancy!

The Brown Recluse earned its name "Recluse" because they seek out-of-the-way places to live. Most Brown Recluse bites occur when they are trapped between an object and skin, not because they are aggressive.

However, in the unlikely event the Brown Recluse spider does envenomate you, it might cause an extremely nasty wound. Ninety percent of the time the wound will heal by itself. Ten percent of the time medical care is needed and antibiotics will usually heal the bite completely. Only three percent of the time will surgery or a skin graft be needed. A Brown Recluse bite is usually described as a "bull's-eye" with a pale center surrounded by a reddened and puffy area. There may be a blister in the center that may rupture and leave an open ulcer. This is the part that frequently becomes infected, causing tissue breakdown. Do not delay getting medical help.

All spider bites are poisonous, and yes, the Brown Recluse bite may develop gangrene-like skin-rotting action, accompanied by fever and flu-like symptoms. But it apparently is not deadly and its infamous reputation is unfounded according to the *Journal of Medical Entomology.*

The Hobo Spider: This spider is not native to the U.S. and it has given the Brown Recluse a bad name. Yup. You read right. The Hobo Spider lives mostly in the Pacific Northwest, but can be found as far east as Montana and south into Oregon and Utah. This brown spider has no distinct markings. Like the Brown Recluse, the bite may develop skin-rotting symptoms. The bites may first appear to be nothing more than a mosquito bite, but within thirty-six hours a blister will form, burst open, and leave an oozing ulceration. If the ulceration is in a fatty tissue of the body, healing can take two, even three, years!

The Yellow Sac Spider: This is another spider whose bite has often been blamed on the shy and timid Brown Recluse and there are two species that are found all over the United States. Many experts believe Sac Spiders cause more bites than any other type of spider bite reported. Like the Brown Recluse and the Hobo Spider, if you are bitten by a Yellow Sac, expect burning, redness, swelling, and if the bite becomes infected, skin-rotting reactions.

Since Sac Spiders account for most skin-rotting spider bites, it is good to know that their bites are not as severe as the Hobo or Brown Recluse. You will also usually know when you have been bitten by a Sac Spider, as they usually produce an intense pain like that of a bee or wasp.

Remember, ninety-eight to ninety-nine percent of spider bites are either harmless or will heal themselves. Of the other two to three percent, most of these bites can be treated with antibiotics. Do not delay, though, in seeking medical attention. You definitely do not want to fall into the small percentage of bites that require anti-venom or surgery.

Snake Bites

If it is slimy and slithers, I do not want anything to do with it. When I was in Basic Training I remember a drill sergeant who caught a Black Rat Snake and thought it would be funny to hand it to the "girls" in the squad. We were still "girls," too. We were seventeen to nineteen years young.

Of course, the first three girls he handed the snake to began squealing and screaming like stuck pigs. That irritated me more than the fact that he thought I should also be handed the dad-burn cold and slimy reptile. This farm girl was prepared for his warped humor and fully intended to pop his bubble, though.

Not only did I take that Black Rat Snake from him and smile, I wrapped it around my shoulders and proceeded to finish the next two miles of our road march with my cold-blooded friend. Once we reached our bivouac site, I had no qualms about making it my supper. And, yes, it tasted like

Non-poisonous Western Yellow Ribbon Snake

chicken. I *loved* the look on my drill sergeant's face! NOTE: It is now illegal to kill this beneficial snake in some states.

Fortunately, like spiders, snakes prefer to go the other way when they encounter humans. They only attack when they feel threatened and in the United States there are only a few venomous snakes to worry about.

The most common of these venomous snakes are pit vipers from the family *Crotalidae*, which includes rattlesnakes, copperheads, and cottonmouths. These snakes get their name from the small "pit" between the eye and nostril. Virtually all venomous snakes in the United States carry a neurotoxic, or nerve destroying, venom.

The other family of snakes in the United States that is venomous is the *Elapidae*, which includes the two species of coral snakes we have, mainly in the Southern states. These snakes also deliver a neurotoxin which can cause respiratory paralysis. Quick medical treatment is essential.

Wash the bite with soap and water. Immobilize the bitten area and keep it <u>lower</u> than the heart. Keep the victim as still as possible to slow the spread of venom. Remove any watches, rings, bracelets, or any other restricting items before swelling sets in. Get medical help without delay and within as few minutes as possible, preferably less than thirty minutes. After you have made the victim as comfortable as possible, wash your hands as venom may be on them.

Non-venomous Speckled Kingsnake (also called a Salt 'n Pepper snake). Speckles are light cream color to yellow.

If you cannot reach help in less than thirty minutes, wrap a bandage two to four inches above the bite to slow the venom. Make sure you are NOT cutting off blood flow. You want to be able to easily slide a finger under the bandage. You want to *slow* the venom, *not* stop the blood. If you have a snake bite kit and there is a suction device in it, that may help to draw the venom out. Do NOT use your mouth. Read the following things NOT to do with a snake bite.

Things NOT to do with a Snake Bite

There are actually more things to NOT do with a snake bite, than to do. Do NOT make cuts at the bite and do NOT try to suck the venom out. This might look good in Westerns, but the first is not medically proven and the latter can be dangerous for you. The vessels under your tongue will absorb the toxin almost immediately and spread it through your blood system. And, do not believe everything you see in the movies. Rattlesnakes do not always "rattle" before they strike. Each rattle is actually an indication of the number of times the snake has shed its skin.

Do NOT apply ice or anything cooling to the bite. This may cause more harm than good. Do NOT apply a tourniquet. This cuts blood flow completely and may result in the loss of the bitten limb. Do NOT make an incision in the wound. This has not been proven effective and may actually cause further injury and infection. When you make a cut at any wound site, you are actually opening capillaries, which opens another direct route into the blood stream for the venom. Do NOT do this.

Note: Only about five people die in the United States each year from a snake bite. That is a reassuringly small number compared to the 7,500 people a year who receive a venomous snake bite.

Skunk Spray

What do you do when the pooch does not pay attention and the skunk sprays him? And you, too, if you are walking him? Skip the vinegar, skip the tomato juice. They do not work. Unless, of course, you use the tomato juice in a few Bloody Mary's to help you pass out so you cannot smell yourself. See the recipe chapter for my Best Bloody Mary in the World if you need this "medicine."

Joking aside, you do want to try to clean your pooch because skunk spray not only smells to high heaven, it can burn and cause temporary blindness if it is sprayed in the eyes. Continuously flush the eyes with pure drinking water. After all the flushing, the eyes will be aggravated and will have lost their natural lubricating tears. Putting in some "tear" drops from your First Aid kit will help sooth your pup's eyes after a thorough flushing. My favorites are GenTeal Lubricant Gel Drops. My vet one time actually prescribed these for my cat. I tried them for my dry eyes and I like them also.

For the obnoxious smell of the spray, mix a bottle of hydrogen peroxide, one-fourth cup of baking soda, and a teaspoon of liquid dish detergent. Apply this mixture immediately and bathe the pooch several times. Do not let the mixture set. Mix fresh each time. Repeat as necessary. Trust me, repeating will be necessary.

A product on the market called Tecnu also claims to be able to remove the smell. I do not know if it works for skunk spray, but it does remove the urushiol of poison plants like it advertises, so I would probably give it a try for the skunk eau de parfume, if need be.

Poison Plant Rashes

"Leaves of Three, Leave Them Be"

How many times have I heard that saying growing up? Poison Ivy, Poison Sumac, and Poison Oak compose the poison plant "terrible trinity" in the plant world as far as skin irritation and unpleasantness. These three plants contain an oil called urushiol in the sap. Just lightly brushing the leaves can give some people an itchy, red, blistery rash.

Poison Ivy, in particular, is found from north to south, east to west, and everywhere in between. It can grow in every type of terrestrial habitat; from prairie to swamp and from forest to glade. It can also grow in full sun and full shade.

In keeping with their "terrible trinity" reputation, two of the plants, poison ivy and poison oak, are each identifiable by the fact that they have three divided leaves coming off of the stem. Poison sumac, on the other hand, has a "crown" of three leaves on a stem with typically four to ten more growing down the stem in pairs to the plant stalk.

Poison Ivy, the most common and widespread member of the "terrible trinity" family, can be found growing in almost any environment.

Your best defense against this "terrible trinity" is to avoid them! Wear long sleeves and long pants if you are tromping around in the poison plant patch. Barring that, there are barrier creams on the market which claim to prevent the oil from even causing a rash. I have used them and have not suffered a poison plant rash when doing so. Now, whether that was due to avoidance on my part, or the cream, I do not know.

If you do come in contact with the terrible trinity, it may be anywhere from 24-48 hours after exposure before you notice a reaction. And, the resulting rash may not be in the area which had direct contact with the plant since the hypersensitive body's reaction to these plant oils is a systemic one.

Even though the reaction site may not be the actual immediate exposure site, it is still highly recommended that you wash the affected area immediately with dishwashing liquid to cut the oil. Hand soap is less than efficient in this case. There are also some good products on the market that help to remove the oil. One is called Zanfel and one is the Tecnu mentioned previously. I have personally used both of these products with favorable results.

After you have thoroughly washed the area, wipe it down with alcohol. If a rash does develop, apply cooling compresses, corticosteroid cream or calamine lotion. An antihistamine will help to decrease itching.

Do not apply a benzocaine-based pain reliever. This is an oily based spray used to treat sunburn pain, but it does not work on the terrible trinity's rash. It may also irritate the area further. Stick to "drying" types of remedies when dealing with the terrible trinity.

Further, avoid touching clothes that have come in contact with the plants. The oils can stay in them even through a washing with regular laundry detergent. If your clothes become contaminated, use dishwashing detergent along with your laundry detergent. The dish detergent will actually remove the oil better than the laundry detergent.

Do not ever burn these plants even when you think they might be dead. The oil survives for up to five years before losing its potency and the urushiol can attach to the smoke from the fire. If you inhale the smoke, you may infect your bronchials.

On the positive side, contrary to popular belief, the rash is not contagious once it is on someone's skin and scratching does not cause it to spread. The hypersensitivity reaction of the body itself is what may cause the rash to spread. If you scratch the lesions and open them, you are inviting an infection.

If the rash is severe or interferes with your ability to perform you daily activities, you may need to seek medical attention. You may be prescribed oral corticosteroids or even given a steroid shot.

Nature is fascinating. Growing near poison ivy a lot of the time in the wild is a beautiful plant called Jewel Weed. The oils in this plant are an actual neutralizer of urushiol and provide itch relief reportedly approximately 95% of the time.

Coincidentally, I had poison ivy when I first read about this plant. I tried rubbing the flower and leaves on the rash with no itch relief. Next, I broke open the stem and rubbed the liquid inside on my rash and felt immediate relief that lasted for hours! I am so happy this weed grows on our farm! It is my new favorite weed! It is said to provide relief for stinging nettle, bee stings, and other insect bites as well. Its cousin, the garden variety Impatiens, is said to work in the same way... I will be planting Impatiens next year.

Stinging Nettle

There is another plant that can cause a very painful stinging sensation if touched incorrectly and this is Stinging Nettle. This plant hurts! These needles can poke through gloves and jeans to deliver their sting. If you accidentally touch Stinging Nettle, you will know it. The site will sting for quite a long time, sometimes up to an hour or two later, depending on how deep the "needles" poked you. Treatment is simply a good hydracortisone cream or antihistaminic cream.

For the sake of research for this book (I am sooooooo dedicated), I went out and stuck myself with stinging nettle to see if Jewel Weed would provide relief as I had read. It did provide relief. Not as dramatically immediate as for my poison ivy itch and chigger bites, but it did - in a very short matter of seconds - calm the pain considerably.

As incongruous as it sounds, this "meanie" of a plant is edible and has a flavor similar to spinach. I even saw a chef collecting it on one of those fancy cooking shows one time!

It is noted that it should not be consumed if it is "flowering" or "seeding." During this stage Stinging Nettle can irritate the urinary tract. No kidding? I think I will just stick to spinach.

Notice the sharp "needles" on the underside of the leaves and the stem. This plant is just plain mean!

Virginia Creeper

Virginia Creeper is another plant that can cause skin dermatitis. In many parts of the country it is called poison ivy or "five-leaved" ivy, but it is not an ivy at all. It is a member of the grapevine family. In some gardens it is used as decoration due to the beautiful red it turns in the autumn.

This plant grows in many of the same areas as poison ivy, however, the Virginia Creeper sap and berries contain oxalate crystals, not urushiol. The crystals are needle-shaped and can irritate the skin, mouth, tongue, and throat, resulting in throat swelling, breathing difficulties, burning pain, and stomach upset.

The berries are poisonous to humans and may be fatal if eaten. In general, it is wise to not mess with things you are not sure what they are. This goes for plants, mushrooms, fruits, berries, or anything you see in the wild when camping.

Virginia Creeper on the ground in the Spring. In the Autumn this plant turns a beautiful ruby red color. Some people actually use it as an ornamental "ivy" it is so pretty.

They may be okay or they may be poisonous. It is best to be safe rather than sorry in any situation, but especially when camping. Most campsites are a considerable distance away from a hospital or medical aid. This is part of a campground's appeal. They are far from civilization.

This means, you have to be smart. Do not fool with anything that you do not absolutely know for sure what it is and what it can do to you if you mess with it. This is just common sense. A trait that comes in handy when camping for pleasure.

Below: Orange and yellow spotted Jewel Weed provides instant ivy, oak, and creeper itch relief. It is also works for insect bites, bee stings, and stinging nettle. It grows in moist, shaded areas.

Hummingbirds love this beneficial flower!

General First Aid

For any First Aid, using any remedy or drug, ALWAYS read the package instructions for correct dosage and warnings. Even if you think, "Well, I've used this before," it is a good thing to re-read the package. Manufacturers frequently come up with "new and improved" items. That "new and improved" ingredient may be something you are allergic to! Better safe than sorry.

Sunburn

First aid for sunburn should not even be needed. There are way too many effective sunblocks on the market these days for anyone to get a sunburn. However, I have light skin and have had a bad sunburn or two and I know someone reading this book will get one. Maybe even me once again, don' cha know.

If you do get a sunburn, a benzocaine-based spray will relieve some of the pain. But this is not my favorite remedy. My grandmother used to bathe me in white household vinegar. This was before sunblock and is a very cooling remedy. (Yeah, I know - "before sun block" - means old.)

The tannic acid in tea is also soothing for sunburn. Steep a large pot of very strong tea, from tea bags (not instant), and put it in the refrigerator or freezer to cool. Soak cloths in the tea and apply to the burn. You can also apply the cold tea bags to the burned area.

Milk also works to take the heat out of a burn. I once mixed my brewed tea with my milk and soaked my rags in the mixture before applying. I think it was the quickest relief I have ever felt from a sunburn. And that was my Florida beach burn! Or was it my Gulfport, Mississippi, burn???

Aloe vera gel, oatmeal mixed with raw egg whites, cucumbers, and raw potatoes are also some good home remedies depending on what you have on hand.

Cooling or inflammation reducing store products that may be used include Noxema, Milk of Magnesia, Vagisil, Pepto-Bismol, and good ole Preparation H. I know they are not advertised for sunburn relief, but sunburn causes inflammation of the skin, so to speak. These anti-inflammatory items reduce that inflammation.

Be careful to read the ingredients of any store bought remedy. Some of them, even the ones with the wonderful aloe vera gel, contain alcohol. Alcohol is a drying agent. It will dry out your skin and increase peeling. Skip the alcohol with a sunburn.

If the sunburn victim can take aspirin, ibuprofen, or acetaminophen, these will also help reduce the inflammation and ease the pain. Take them with water. Lots of water. Water will speed the healing process and replenish your skin. Again, though, your best bet is to not stay in the sun over long and to wear a sun block!

Do not; however, give aspirin to a child under the age of nineteen without a doctor's knowledge. It can cause Ryes Syndrome, a lethal disease.

========================

Always read and follow the instructions on any box of any type of medication - even over the counter remedies! New information comes out all the time. Stay up to date.

Blisters

I am publishing a disclaimer right here and right now. Depending on which source you go to, some say to pop the blister, some say to leave the blister alone. Some say to leave the skin on. Some say to remove the skin. I will provide both First Aid treatment methods and you can choose which one you prefer. (NOTE: Blisters caused by thermal burns should NOT be burst. See the following subject, "First Degree and Thermal Burns.")

Blisters are fluid filled sacs under your skin. They can be caused by sunburn or by friction on your skin. If a shoe or boot does not fit correctly, many times you can get a blister on your heel. If you are wearing damp socks, you can rub a blister on your foot. Keep your feet dry!

I have been retired for several years now and I still love my Army green wool socks! If I am in jeans and tennis shoes on the hottest day of summer, I will have my wool socks on. Not cotton. The wool just seems to keep my feet cooler and I know it "wicks" the moisture away from my feet and keeps them dryer. I love woolies! My feet are warm in winter and cool in summer. Anyway, back to blisters...

The fluid inside a blister is lymph fluid and forms a protective barrier between the raw damaged inner skin layers and the outer skin layers. Since the skin covering a blister is providing protection, it can be left intact.

If the area might be subject to further irritation and susceptible to bursting or ripping on its own, you may want to pop the blister. To do this, puncture the base of the blister with a sterile needle. To sterilize the needle, rub alcohol over it or place it in your lighter flame for a few seconds.

After you have drained the blister, smooth an antibiotic cream over it and pad it with moleskin, 2nd Skin, gauze, or a large bandage. Some say to remove the skin, some say do not. I am going with the middle road here.

If the skin has a tear in it that might rip further into your skin area, you might remove the blister "roof." If you do remove the skin, make sure you keep it sterile and protected.

If there is not a tear in the blister that might cause further injury, you may decide to not remove the skin over the blister. After all, this skin does provide a protective layer for the underlying skin and will help prevent infection.

First Degree and Thermal Burns

Burns from a fire, boiling water, or steam are called
thermal burns and are extremely painful. If you are thermally
burned, remove the source of the burn. (I know, *that part* is
reflexive and probably happens immediately!) Cool the area
with running cold water for at least ten minutes. Do NOT
apply butter, grease, cream, or any other ointment on these
types of burns.

Do NOT break any blisters that form over a burn.
Remove all jewelry and keep the area cool. Place a padded
cloth over the burn. If a blister over a burn does rip or tear,
treat it as mentioned previously in the "Blisters" section.

I have worked as a cook in my husband's grill for
many a shift. And, I have burned myself once or twice cooking
over the years. Ice in a sandwich bag is a wonderful cooling
treatment. Be sure to place a towel between your burn and the
bag. You do not want the ice to "freeze" or further damage the
skin around the area.

I have gone to bed holding a frozen roll of hamburger
with my hand elevated on a pillow to relieve the throbbing. I
have gone to bed cuddling frozen peas. My husband says I am
"dangerous" in a kitchen. I say I am just enthusiastic. Light
hearted as that sounds, I do take burns seriously. If not treated
properly, they can cause serious scarring.

Superficial Bleeding

Bicycle accidents. Thorn bushes. Sharp knives.
Stumbling over a rock on a trail. Going to the shower house
and tripping over a guide wire in the dark. The opportunities to
skin yourself up on a camping trip are numerous. Fortunately,
it does not happen all that often. But, kids will be kids, no
matter what their age and we do get cuts, skins, and scrapes.

Clean the wound gently with soap and water. Do not

scrub the wound. If gravel or other debris is lodged in the skin, flush it out with plenty of clean drinking water. Douse with hydrogen peroxide or other antiseptic wash. Cover with an antibiotic ointment and bandage.

Unless the wound becomes infected, it should not be necessary to apply hydrogen peroxide multiple times. Doing so is detrimental to healing. The hydrogen peroxide "bubbles" away the very fragile and newly-formed healing skin cells.

Bandage Wounds

For generations, mothers have told us that cuts and scrapes heal faster when they are uncovered, opened to the air, can dry and form a scab. Now the medical world tells us a covered wound heals faster.

A bandage keeps the area moist and healing skin cells and tissue can form faster without having to work under a scab. Plus, a scab can lead to a scar. Bandaging the wound also prevents any further infection from dirt or germs. Sorry, Mom.

Sugar or Honey Will Work in a Pinch

After you have cleaned and flushed the wound, if you are out of antibacterial ointment, grab some sugar. Seriously. Sugar is a proven antimicrobial agent. Just place some white sugar or honey on the cut. The sugar will melt/dissolve, mix with the fluids of your wound, and inhibit bacterial growth. Yep. Plain ole sugar or honey will work in a pinch.

Simple Fractures

If you think a limb might be broken or fractured, splint it and immobilize the limb to prevent further injury. Use a tree branch, a cane, a tent pole - whatever is available. You can even use the victim's own body.

If the arm is fractured, place the arm over the chest and tie it to the body with strips of cloth that are long enough to go around the entire torso. If it is the leg, strap the broken leg to the uninjured leg at different locations.

The joint above and below the site of the fracture must be immobilized. Never attempt to straighten the fracture! This should only be done by medical professionals.

Splint the limb as it lays - do not move it around - and seek medical attention immediately.

Heat Injuries

Young children, older adults, obese people, persons with chronic illnesses, and those drinking alcoholic beverages are at increased risk of heat injury.

Prevention: We go camping to play. But all play and no rest can lead to a heat injury. If you have been out on the lake or anywhere in the sun for a long period of time, take a shade break! Play early in the morning or late in the afternoon, not when the sun is directly overhead. Drink plenty of water, skip the alcohol, and eat. You have to replace the salt and the electrolytes in your body that you sweat out and the "drinks" on the market, while helpful, are not the "be all and end all" of heat injury prevention.

On hot days, 85 degrees Fahrenheit or higher, you need to be drinking at least one quart of water an hour. If the temperature is 90 degrees Fahrenheit or above, that water intake needs to increase to at least two quarts an hour.

Heat Cramps: There are actually three types of heat injury. The least serious is heat cramps. This is exactly what it sounds like. You will experience muscle cramps in the arms and legs, perhaps even the abdomen. These cramps will be accompanied by heavy sweating and hopefully, extreme thirst.

Get to a shady area and loosen any tight clothing and start drinking plenty of cool water slowly and continuously.

In most cases, this should do the trick and you should start to feel better. If not, you might have heat exhaustion.

Heat Exhaustion: With heat exhaustion, there is a good chance you will have cramps and heavy sweating. Heat exhaustion symptoms may also include headache, dizziness, loss of appetite, nausea, vomiting, chills, shallow and/or rapid breathing, disorientation, confusion, low blood pressure, and maybe even tingling in your extremities. Your body temperature, while possibly elevated, will be less than 104 degrees Fahrenheit. Usually your mental status will be normal with heat exhaustion. So pay attention to what your body is feeling!

Again, move to a shady area and in this case, remove as much clothing as possible. At the very least, remove any socks and shoes and hats. Elevate your legs. If someone is available to help you, they should administer cool compresses to your body. Keep the compresses changed so they are continuously cool.

While all this is happening, you should be drinking cool water continuously and slowly. If you experience no relief, seek medical attention.

Heat Stroke: Sometimes a victim of heat stroke will experience headache, dizziness, nausea, stomach pains, confusion, weakness, seizures, a weak or rapid pulse/heartbeat, and shallow breathing. Fainting may occur and the blood pressure may be either low or elevated. Skin will become red and flushed while feeling dry to the touch and sweating almost always stops. This inability to sweat will increase the body's core temperature to 104 degrees Fahrenheit and over.

Changes in the victim's mental status such as confusion, personality changes, or even coma may occur. Seek medical attention immediately.

Hopefully, a heat stroke victim will recognize these symptoms before they pass out! Pay attention to your body. If you are not thirsty, drink anyway. If you are not hungry, eat anyway. Your body is made up of mostly water and needs to be hydrated to function optimally. If your body cannot sweat, you are not hydrated. Heat stroke is a medical emergency!

Get the victim to a shady area and remove clothing. Start cooling the victim as instructed with heat exhaustion. If you can fan them while applying the cool compresses, all the better. Elevate their legs and massage their hands and feet. If they are conscious, get them to start drinking cool water slowly. Do not let them gulp it or they will just throw it back up. Conscious or unconscious, seek medical help without hesitation and immediately!

Hyponatremia: When I passed out in the military during hot weather training I had hyponatremia, not heat stroke. Remember, I had drank copious amounts of water all day long, but I had not eaten anything. Nor had I drank a sports drink containing electrolytes. Hyponatremia, also called water intoxication, is the result of drinking excessive amounts of water and literally "flushing out" your body's electrolytes.

The result is lowered sodium and other critical electrolytes our bodies need to function at optimum capacity. Marathon runners, long-distance and extreme athletes make up the most common victims of hyponatremia. Military personnel are also at risk due to intense training programs.

The symptoms are similar to dehydration. You may experience nausea, muscle cramps, disorientation, and slurred speech. If you make the erroneous assumption you are dehydrated, knowing you have been drinking water, and you drink even more water you will have just increased the seriousness of the hyponatremia, also called hyper-hydration.

At its most serious, hyponatremia can cause seizures, coma, and even death. Medical attention is critical. To prevent hyponatremia, eat meals and snacks on those hot summer days. Skip the salt pills. The military has even stopped using these. It is better to eat sensibly. If you are on a low-sodium diet, it is imperative you pay attention to what your body is telling you. If your urine is dark yellow, you probably are dehydrated. If, however, your urine is clear and you are exhibiting the above mentioned symptoms, you may need some food intake.

Individuals who are dieting radically and incorrectly need to be aware they are making themselves susceptible to hyponatremia. If you have been drinking huge amounts of water to curb hunger and drastically cutting food intake to cut calories, you may become a hyponatremia case waiting to happen. Moderation in everything is the best avenue of diet to follow. Drink slowly all day long, eat regularly, and exercise.

Cold Weather Illness and Injury

Cold Weather Illness: It is not the cold environment that causes respiratory infections such as the flu or pneumonia. These illnesses are caused by viruses and bacteria which thrive in warm indoor environments - our houses in the winter.

But, if you have spent the weekend camping in cold weather, your body has possibly had to work overtime to keep warm. If you shivered at all, this means you body was trying to stay warm. All that extra work can weaken your immune system and viruses and bacteria can have a heyday.

Stay warm and dry when camping in cold weather. When you return home, do not crank your thermostat up in reaction to a cool weekend. Cranking the heat will encourage viruses and bacteria to breed, increasing your risk of catching a cold or something worse.

Should you come down with a cold weather illness, cover your mouth when coughing or sneezing. Wash your hands frequently. Try to avoid contact with anyone who has an active respiratory or gastrointestinal infection. And the best advice: Wash your hands...wash your hands...wash your hands.

If you have a cold weather illness, keep a disinfectant handy. Frequently clean the telephone, the toilet handle, water faucet handles, the refrigerator door, and all door knobs.

Cold Weather Injury: Two of the most common cold weather injuries are Hypothermia and Frostnip.

Hypothermia: In the section covering cold weather clothes layering, hypothermia was covered in some detail. It was mentioned there specifically because a person sweating under too many layers of clothes, even in balmy weather, can succumb to hypothermia. Sweat conducts heat away from your body 25 times faster than air. It is essential to stay dry.

If someone is "umbling" in cool weather (stumbling, mumbling, fumbling, or grumbling), they may have hypothermia. Other symptoms include violent shivering, loss of motor coordination, muscle rigidity, pale skin, dilated pupils, decreased pulse rate, and possible loss of consciousness.

Get the victim dry and warm. If conscious, give them hot liquids and food. Do not give them alcohol, caffeine, or tobacco. If the person has severe hypothermia and cannot eat, give them warm sugar water. Diluted gelatin that is part sugar and part protein is an excellent choice. It must be diluted. If they cannot digest food, they will not be able to digest fully concentrated gelatin.

After the person is dry, apply dry heat to major artery areas: The neck, the armpits, and the groin. Seek medical attention immediately.

Frostnip: Symptoms of frostnip include white, waxy skin and numbness. Ears, cheeks, fingers, and toes are most likely to be frostnipped. The top layer of skin will feel hard and rubbery. Frostnip is a milder form of frostbite.

To rewarm the skin, immerse the affected part in warm water. This process will be painful as the feeling returns. Make sure the water is between 100-105 degrees Fahrenheit and no warmer. After you have immersed the cold part of the body, the water will cool down and you will have to repeat the procedure several times. You will need to monitor the water to maintain the correct temperature. Do not use dry heat for frostnip or frostbite. Seek medical aid as soon as possible.

First Aid Kit List

_____ First aid instruction book

_____ Band aids and moleskin

_____ Special gauze pads for burns

_____ Adhesive tape

_____ Butterfly bandages

_____ An elastic roll bandage for sprains

_____ Over-the-counter pain reliever

_____ Allergy reliever, such as Benadryl

_____ Nasal spray

_____ Antacids and diarrhea medicine

_____ Syrup of ipecac (induces vomiting)

_____ Anti-bacterial cream

_____ Anti-itching lotion, such as Caladryl

_____ Hydrogen peroxide

_____ Mosquito repellent

_____ Sunscreen and sunburn reliever

_____ Lip balm

_____ Clear fingernail polish

_____ Camphor phynique oil

_____ Athlete's foot treatment and foot powder

_____ Baby Tylenol (if travelling with children)

_____ Zinc oxide

_____ Instant cold pack and heat pack

_____ Topical pain reliever for muscles (Ben-Gay)

_____ Eye drops or liquid tears (GenTeal)

_____ Tick remover, tweezers, scissors

Variable items:

_____

_____

_____

_____

_____

Your first aid kit could contain many other items, including a snake bite kit depending on the countryside where you camp. If you have a medical condition that might require hospitalization, you should also have your medical information and a medical list with all your prescriptions noted. Do not forget to add your allergies to any medical list.

Medical Condition Summarization:

_____

_____

_____

_____

_____

_____

_____

_____

_____

_____

_____

_____

_____

_____

_____

Photo by Steve Allee

This Great Blue Heron on Truman Lake in
Missouri is just waiting for supper to swim by.
It is his home, help keep it G.R.E.E.N.

Chapter Five
~ Dessert ~
Campfire Cuisine

Anyone Can Be a Campfire Gourmet

If you have paid any attention to my chapter titles, you have figured out by now that I am fixated on food. One of the greatest joys of camping to me is the cooking and grilling.

Everything just tastes better when eaten in the great outdoors, especially if it has been cooked over an open fire. I readily admit that my husband and I eat better when camping than we do at home. It is just more fun to cook. (Sorry, honey.)

I am not afraid of experimenting with my meals and hopefully you, too, will feel adventurous. The following recipes are my own. I have taken other recipes that I liked and adapted them to my husband's and my own preferences. I highly encourage you to do the same.

No Lunch Recipes Found Here

You will note I have not one lunch recipe listed. Lunch is catch as catch can in my camper. That means, grab a hotdog or a sandwich. I play during the day, I do not cook lunch!

Breakfast Recipes

Breakfast should be a party, not something to dread. (I am NOT a morning person.) My breakfasts tend to be very easy to cook and very easy to clean up after. Most of my recipes are all geared toward two people. Increase amounts accordingly.

One Pan Breakfast Bash

1 cup cubed ham (about 1/2 inch cubes)
1/2 cup cubed Velveeta cheese
3 tablespoons butter
1/4 cup milk
5-6 eggs depending on size
1/8 cup chopped onion or chives
1/2 cup chopped tomato,
      preferably juiceless and seedless
Pepper and Seasoned salt to taste

Place you skillet on a medium fire, either inside in the camper or on a campfire, whichever you prefer. Put the ham, two tablespoons of the butter, and the onion in the skillet and brown them until the onion becomes soft. Add your eggs, milk, and your third tablespoon of butter and stir until the eggs are mixed and cook until they are almost done.

Add your tomatoes at the very end, giving them just enough time to get hot. You do not want them cooked to mush. Add some pepper and seasoned salt, and you have a scrambled omelet worth waking up to make!

Breakfast Bash Variations

If you want to use bacon or sausage instead of ham, just be sure to drain the grease and maybe cut back on the butter some.

Also, do not be afraid to experiment. Adding fresh asparagus or spinach to these eggs are two of my favorite variations. Add mushrooms! Switch cheeses. Use Farmer's cheese on occasion. Ever buy some of that fake crabmeat in the store? It is good in this recipe also. Want a touch of heat in your scrambled omelet? Add some hot sauce or cayenne pepper. Mix it up with all kinds of herbs. There are no limits.

Biscuits and Gravy

1 lb. sausage, browned and crumbled
3 cups milk
Estimated 3 heaping tablespoons flour

Go ahead and leave your sausage in the skillet with the grease. Add enough flour to totally coat the sausage crumbles and soak up any grease. You want your flour to almost be "dry" again in the skillet. (If the sausage had a LOT of grease, you might want to drain it down to about two tablespoons.) Let the flour get slightly brown **before** you add the milk. Stir continuously until gravy is thickened. Salt and pepper to taste. Serve over biscuits or toasted bread. (See homemade and easy biscuit recipe on page 154.)

Pancakes

My husband loves pancakes and French toast and I try to make one of these choices for him at least once during our trips. If I make French toast, I almost always use Texas toast for the bread. Recently, though, we have tried and liked the cinnamon toast that you buy in loaves in the store. There are other flavored loaves, such as blueberry, available now. We will eventually get around to trying them all I am sure.

As far as the pancakes go, there is not much variation to them. I usually cheat and use a box mix anyway. However, his syrup and topping is another story entirely.

On our camping trips we splurge and either use real maple syrup - not the fake colored corn syrup maple-flavored stuff - but the real stuff, or I make a topping from scratch. My husband's favorite recipe uses peaches. I prefer apples and it is the same recipe, just using different fresh fruits.

Peachy Keen Pancake Topping

2 cups peeled and thinly sliced peaches
1/2 stick butter
3/4 cup brown sugar
Cinnamon and Nutmeg to taste

Melt your butter in a sauce pan over a medium heat. Roll and coat your peaches in the brown sugar. Drop them in the sauce pan and cook until your brown sugar melts into a syrup and the peaches are soft. Do not burn! Drizzle over hot, buttered pancakes or French toast. Sprinkle a little cinnamon and powdered sugar over the top and enjoy.

We have also used apples and bananas for this recipe with great results. I would imagine fresh pears or plums would work as well. Now that I have thought of them, I am sure going to try them!

Get really, really decadent and pour some warm caramel and sprinkle chopped pecans or walnuts over the top of your pancakes.

Sugar Free Peachy Keen Pancake Topping

2 cups peeled and sliced peaches
Sugar-free sweetener to taste (3-4 tablespoons)
1/2 stick butter
1 cup water
2 tablespoons corn starch mixed separately into
          1/2 cup cold water until smooth

Boil the peaches until soft. Add sweetener and butter to taste. Once the peaches are done, mix your corn starch and cold water and add the corn starch mixture a little at a time, drizzling it into the hot mix and stirring continuously. Turn the fire off and let the mixture thicken.

Okay, I know I said I usually cheat and use a box pancake mix, but on occasion I do actually spoil my husband and give him homemade pancakes. When I do, I use the following recipe.

Very Versatile Pancakes

1 large egg
1 cup milk
1 tablespoon lemon juice (or white vinegar)
1 cup all purpose flour (can use 1/2 whole wheat)
1 tablespoon sugar
1 teaspoon baking powder
1/2 teaspoon baking soda
1/2 teaspoon salt
2 tablespoons melted butter or vegetable oil

Mix the milk and lemon in a cup and let it stand until it thickens. In a bowl, whisk dry ingredients together. In a separate bowl, add the egg and melted butter/oil to the milk mix. Create a "well" in the center of the dry ingredients and pour in the milk mix. Whisk gently until combined. There should still be lumps.

Heat your griddle to medium heat and coat with oil. (To test your griddle, take a pinch of flour and drop into the oil. The flour should immediately sizzle.) Pour pancake mix by 1/4 cup onto the heated griddle. Cook pancake until large bubbles appear on the top. They should be puffed and dry around the edge. Flip the pancake and cook lightly until golden brown. It won't take long on the second side.

These pancakes are great! And, remember I said, "versatile?" Well, here is the versatile part. If you do not have lemon or vinegar, do not panic. The milk by itself works just fine. No baking soda? It is still alright. You do need the baking powder, though. Want a thinner pancake? Just add water.

Pancake Variations

Want a really moist pan "cake" pancake? Decrease milk by 1/2 and add 1/2 cup applesauce with a little cinnamon. Substitute buttermilk and leave out the lemon juice/vinegar. Use a flavored yogurt instead of the milk. It's all good!

Add 1/2 cup of any fruit and/or 1/4 cup of any nuts you like. Go ahead and add them both! Substitute whole wheat flour for all or part of the white flour, use molasses or brown sugar instead of the white sugar. Be adventurous!

Make things ahead of time! Especially the following three: Baked Potatoes, Biscuit Dough, and Noodles

Potatoes: Bake a couple of extra for dinner. Leftover sliced, chopped, or mashed spuds are a great breakfast food.

Breakfast Spuds

2 large, leftover and cold, baked potatoes, cubed
1 medium onion, chopped
2 tablespoons butter or oil or bacon fat
Salt and pepper to taste

Heat oil in skillet. Add potatoes and onion. Cook until potatoes are crispy on the outside and hot on the inside. Since your potatoes are already cooked, this does not take very long.

Or, mash the potatoes, add one egg and one teaspoon of flour, and you can make potato cakes and lightly fry them. Grill your chopped onion a tiny bit first, or not. Your choice. You might like your onion a little crunchy.

Using baking grease from the bacon you cooked for breakfast? Crumble up a couple of slices of bacon into the potato cakes for a big boost of bacon flavor. (This is my favorite extra in these spuds.)

Dough: My next recipe is a great one! You can make this dough ahead of time at home, put it in a plastic food storage bag, refrigerate it, and bring it along on your camping trip to have homemade biscuits from scratch the easy way!

Buttermilk Refrigerator Biscuits

1 package (1/4 ounce) dry yeast
1/2 cup warm water   2 cups buttermilk
5 cups flour   3 teaspoons baking powder
1 teaspoon salt   1 teaspoon baking soda
3 tablespoons sugar   3/4 cup solid shortening

Dissolve yeast in warm water to proof and cover loosely; set aside. (Make sure your yeast is not out of date.) Add a sprinkle of sugar for the yeast to "feed" on.

Sift together flour, baking powder, salt, soda, and sugar. Cut in shortening. Add buttermilk and mix. Add water and yeast mixture; mix until moistened. Cover bowl and refrigerate until needed.

When ready to use, preheat oven to 375 degrees Fahrenheit. Take amount of dough needed, roll on floured board to a generous 1/2 inch thickness and cut with biscuit cutter (or a glass). You can also put flour on your hands and pull chunks off and press them into the right size for baking.

Place them on a baking or cookie sheet with an inch or so between them. Bake betweeen 12 - 15 minutes.

Noodles: One other thing to make ahead of time to take with you in a plastic food storage bag is some fettuccini or macaroni. To keep your pasta from becoming one glutenous lump: After you drain the hot water from the pasta, rinse it with cool water. Put it into your bag and add a couple of table-spoons of olive oil. Swish the oil around until all of the pasta is lightly coated and refrigerate.

Breakfast Fettuccini

2 lightly packed cups cooked fettuccini
2 eggs
1 tablespoon butter
6 slices bacon or 1/2 lb. sausage or ham
1/2 cup milk or half and half or cream
1/2 cup grated Italian cheese mix
1/4 cup chopped onion
Salt, pepper, and garlic flakes to taste

Cook your meat in a skillet. Remove meat. If there is a lot of grease, drain it down to approximately one tablespoon. Add chopped onion and cook until translucent. (If using fresh garlic - add with onion.)

Return meat to skillet. Toss the noodles into the skillet and warm them. In a separate bowl, mix eggs, milk, and butter. (If using onion or garlic flakes instead of fresh - add the flakes into the milk mixture at this time.) Pour mixture over noodles and meat. Lightly toss until eggs are done.

Sprinkle the grated Italian cheese mix over the top of the entire meal and serve.

This recipe is easy to increase. For each cup of noodles added, add one egg, 1 teaspoon butter, 1/8 cup milk, a little more cheese and some onion.

Fresh green beans and new baby potatoes bought at a road-side stand, seasoned with onions and bacon, then cooked right in the fire. It doesn't get any easier or taste any better!

Dinner Recipes

Steve's Texas Squealer Grilled Hamburgers

1 lb. hamburger (Use 80-20 or 70-30 for best flavor.)
1/2 lb. ground smoked ham
2 eggs beaten
1 tablespoon Tone's Roasted Garlic
1 tablespoon Worcestershire Sauce   <u>Toppings</u>
2 teaspooons Seasoned salt   Bacon
1 teaspoon Cumin   Butter
1/8 teaspoon Liquid Smoke   Cheese

Place smoked ham in chunks in a food processor and pulse until ham is ground to a consistency comparable to the hamburger. Add to the hamburger along with the eggs and the rest of the ingredients. Mix just until blended well. Do not overmix or you will make the hamburger tough. Shape into 1/2 pound patties and grill. When mostly done, spread butter over the patty and top with smoked cheddar cheese and/or bacon strips. Serve on a bun lightly buttered and toasted on the grill.

The following Foil Wrapped Recipes are so easy to do, we almost always have them the first night. Prepare your packets at home and place them in the cooler for a meal ready to cook upon arrival at the campground. Keep in mind that almost all of my recipes are geared for two people. Add or subtract amounts depending on how many people you are cooking for.

CAUTION!

Be careful when opening the foil! Burning hot steam will escape! Poke a few holes in the foil first, to let most of the steam out, before actually opening it all the way.

Foil-Wrapped Hamburger and Veggies

Hamburger	Onion
Potatoes	Mrs. Dash
Carrots	Butter

You will need two 24-36" lengths of aluminum foil to make cooking packets. Make meatballs out of hamburger and season to taste. I like to use Mrs. Dash Original seasoning or Morton's Nature's Seasoning for this recipe.

Use about 1/2 pound of hamburger for each person. This amount will make approximately three to four meatballs for each aluminum foil packet. Place meat balls on the foil.

Wash and cut into bite sized pieces one large potato or two small to medium-sized potatoes. Divide evenly. Add carrots, celery, onion, and any other fresh vegetable you have on hand and want to include. Drop a big dollop of butter on top of meat and veggies. Sprinkle more Mrs. Dash or other favorite seasoning on the veggies.

Wrap the meat and veggies inside the foil tightly. Fold the foil so that the butter does not leak. Place the foil packets on the coals of your campfire. Turn the packet frequently so that the side resting on the coals does not burn. Sometimes, if my coals are really hot, I will double wrap my food in two layers of aluminum foil. Depending on how hot your coals are, your meal should be ready in twenty to thirty minutes.

Hamburger is easy to use the first night. I have, however, used chicken bites and venison bites for this same recipe. I have even left out the potatoes and carrots and used only fresh green beans, broccoli, and fresh asparagus.

I especially like to use the items my husband and I have purchased when we have stopped at a roadside fresh vegetable market on the way to our destination. And, if you prefer, skip the veggies altogether.

Missouri Wine-Flavored Meat in Foil

1/4 cup Missouri red wine (One you like to drink!)
3/4 cup catsup or barbecue sauce
    (Or a combination of both.)
1/4 cup all purpose flour
2 pounds round steak or other red meat
1 large onion, sliced
1 tablespoon lemon juice

 Tear off about four feet of aluminum foil and fold double. Combine your catsup/barbecue sauce, wine, and flour. Spoon half into the center of the foil. Put the steak on top and season with your favorite seasoning (for this I like a Tone's Roasted Garlic and/or Chipotle seasoning). Cover with the onion slices, the other half of the mix, sprinkle with lemon juice, and seal the aluminum foil.
 Place over the coals on grill wires and cook for forty-five minutes to an hour, making sure you turn the foil on occasion (this means frequently) to keep the side closest to the coals from burning.

To clean cast iron pots and pans, toss them right on the fire. Once all the food has turned to ash, let the pan cool then dust out the ashes. Very, <u>very</u> lightly coat the inside with oil to prevent rust until ready for next use.

Show Me Meat In Foil Variations

Here is the fun part with my recipes. Switch the red wine for white, use chicken or pork chops instead of round steak, change the catsup or barbecue sauce to Italian salad dressing, and you have a whole new recipe! With all the seasonings in the dressing, you will not need any other type of seasoning.

Want a really tender cut of meat? Buy a pork tenderloin and wrap it whole in the foil. Keep a close watch on the coals when using tenderloins. They will cook quickly, about 20 to 30 minutes is more than enough. Tenderloin can become dry very quickly.

Baked Potatoes

Poke a couple of baking potatoes several times - deeply - with a fork. Wrap them in foil, drop them onto the coals, and you can have a baked potato with your meat in the foil. Depending on the size of the potatoes, they may need a whole hour. Do these first if they are large. Also, be sure to add a couple of extra potatoes to the fire so you can make hash brown cubes or potato cakes for breakfast the next morning.

Shagbark Hickory Nuts. These nuts are hard to crack open!

Venison Marinade

Cover venison totally with milk and let marinade two hours to overnight. That is it. This will take the "wild" taste out without ruining the wonderful flavor of the venison. Some people will tell you to use vinegar. Do not do it! If you are a dedicated "foodie" like me, you will be able to taste the vinegar after the venison is cooked. If you want a German "sauerbraten" flavor, by all means, use vinegar. If you just want to enjoy the flavor of the meat, use milk!

And, do not use salt in this marinade. Venison does not have a lot of fat in it and can easily become dry when cooked. Salt will pull the blood from the venison and make it an even dryer piece of meat. One-half hour to two hours before cooking venison, switch to the red meat marinade.

The best way to cook venison tenderloins: After marinating, season lightly with salt and pepper. Stab the steaks onto your marshmallow wire and hold over the coals for approximately 3-4 minutes. Eat straight off the wires. Yum!

Honey bees go through a long process to make the honey we enjoy. Some farmers even "rent" colonies of honey bees to pollinate their crops in some areas of the country. Honey bees are a critical part of the world's food chain - which includes humans. If you do not absolutely need to use pesticides, don't. Buy organic and support farmers who do not use chemical pestiticides. Albert Einstein once predicted that if bees were to become extinct, man would follow only a few years later. Honey bees are essential insects. They are vital to bio diversity. Bee expert Joergen Tautz says, "Bees are not only working for *our* welfare, they are also a perfect indicator of the state of the environment. We should take note."

Mellody's Red Meat Marinade

In a plastic bag mix:
    1/2 cup Worcestershire's sauce
    1 tablespoon sesame seed oil
    2 tablespoons Tone's Chipotle seasoning
    1/4 teaspoon smoke flavoring
    1/8 teaspoon cumin
    1/8 teaspoon paprika
    Pepper to taste
    No salt! (There is plenty in the
                Worcestershire sauce.)
    1/2 cup red wine is optional
        (It must be good drinking wine.
        If you do not like it to drink,
        do not use it to cook with!)

Plus, if you do not like to use alcohol, use 1/4 cup of sugar free fruit jam. Plum, cherry, grape... Pick your fave and go for it. Or just use 1 tablespoon of brown sugar. Your choice.

Add your venison or beef to the bag, swish it around and make sure the meat is generously covered. Let the meat marinate for at least 1/2 hour, preferably closer to two hours. Grill meat on an open fire, serve, and enjoy.

Many of the Missouri Pecans are certified organic American Native Northern Pecans, the best kind! You can see the "World's Largest Pecan" outside the town of Brunswick, MO. It is a nutty, but true, claim. The best time to visit is during the Pecan Festival in October.

White Meat Marinade Harmony

1/2 cup Worcestershire Chicken sauce
           (This is white Worcestershire.)
1 tablespoon walnut or grape oil
2 tablespoons Tone's Roasted Garlic seasoning
1/8 teaspoon smoke flavoring
1/2 cup white wine is optional
           as is a light fruit sugar free jam,
                 such as white grape or peach.

Add chicken, fish, or pork and let marinade for the magical 1/2 to two hours. Grill meat on an open fire. Grill fish with the skin side down.

Again, I will add or subtract seasonings and flavors as my taste buds desire. Sometimes I like my marinade smoky and sometimes I want it a little sweeter. It just depends on my mood. None of my recipes are carved in stone, so please, finesse them to your taste bud's desires!

Notice our smoker is on hand and the fact that the left awning pole is lower than the right.

From My Family to Your Family

Move over canned baked beans with a certain Irish Setter in their commercials. My Bodacious Baked Beans are moving in. My stepmom taught me this recipe that has been in her family for years (in a considerably larger amount) and I think they are the best baked beans I have ever tasted.

My stepmom's sister and husband used to own a restaurant and served these beans there. When they sold their restaurant, family rumor has it that the buyers had a clause put in the contract that my stepaunt and stepuncle could not operate another restaurant within a fifty mile radius for five years (they cooked some good food in their restaurant!) And even more specifically, they could not reveal their baked bean recipe to any other restaurant. That is how good these baked beans are! Is this really my family history or a tall tale? You be the judge. I think the recipe will make your mind up easily.

Bodacious "Baked" Beans

1/3 pound bacon, chopped and fried, in your cast iron sauce pan. Drain the grease and add one small chopped onion. Cook until the onion is translucent. Then add:

2 cans pork 'n beans (1 lb. size cans)
3/4 cup catsup (or barbecue sauce)
3/4 cup brown sugar
1 tablespoon + 1 teaspoon prepared mustard
1 tablespoon + 1 teaspoon Worcestershire sauce
1/2 teaspoon liquid smoke
Salt and pepper to taste

Cover and let simmer two hours over the coals or until they are a consistency you like your "baked" beans to be. Stir frequently to keep the beans from sticking to the bottom of the pan and burning.

Grilled Onions in Foil

1 small box or package of
      flavored minute-type rice
2 medium to large onions for slicing
4 tablespoon butter

Cook your rice according to package directions. Slice your onions approximately 1/2 inch thick. Put 1/2 rice mixture on foil. Place onion on top. Pile the rest of the rice on top of the slices and top with a dollop of butter. Wrap foil and grill over coals ten to fifteen minutes until onions are nicely done and sweetly grilled.

As an alternative, you can also use instant stuffing instead of the rice. Or, saute some fresh mushrooms, celery, and lots of garlic in some olive oil, then top the onions with this mix. Add carrot slices or green pepper slices for variation.

Garlic and onion become very sweet and flavorful when prepared this way. My husband likes just the garlic cloves and onions prepared this way, especially with grilled chicken. You could also place your foil in the bottom of your Dutch oven and bake your onions. There is a little more cleanup involved, but your Dutch oven will help keep your onions from burning if your coals are too hot.

Estimating Briquette Temperature

I keep saying, "keep from burning," "if your coals are too hot," etc., etc., etc. I love cooking over coals! I think food tastes so good this way, but you can burn stuff really easily. Coals get white hot. If you cook in coals you must watch the food very carefully! The number of coals you use will determine the heat temperature. Each coal can be counted as approximately 30 degrees Fahrenheit in an enclosed grill.

Grilled Corn on the Cob

This is the only way to cook fresh corn on the cob when camping or grilling at home! Take the ears of corn and peel back the husks, but do not break the husks off. Remove any worms or bad spots and the silk. With the husks still pulled back, soak the corn cobs in cool water at least 20 - 30 minutes, up to eight hours. You want the husks moist, not dry.

While you are soaking the cobs, take some chilled butter and add salt and pepper to taste. If you are feeling adventurous, add some cayenne or chipotle flavoring to your butter. If you do not like it hot, try garlic or onion powder, parsley or other herbs in your butter.

Smear the seasoned butter liberally all over your corn cobs. This will be a sloppy and glumpy mess. Wrap the husks back up around the cob nice and snug. Wrap in foil and place on the grill or directly on the coals. Turn occasionally if on the grill or frequently if on the coals to get all sides evenly done, but not overdone. In 15-20 minutes you will have the absolute best corn on the cob you have ever tasted!

Trash bags might be a camper's favorite commodity! Pillow case, rain poncho, or tent; they have so many uses! Here I used one to cover Champ's travel doggie house during an unexpected light drizzle. This year, since he is now full grown - four feet long and three feet tall - he gets his own "pup" tent. He is spoiled!

Remember those two cold, leftover, baked potatoes that you knew you would need sometime on your camping trip? If you did not use them for breakfast, try the following recipe.

No Mayo Warm Potato Salad

Cube two warm baked potatoes or the leftover and cold baked potatoes you had for supper. (I always leave the skins on, but you can remove the potato skins if you prefer.)

4 slices of bacon, cooked and crumbled
1 small onion
1/2 cup chopped celery
1 tablespoon flour
2 tablespoons vinegar
4 tablespoons water
1 1/2 tablespoon sugar or sweetener

After you have cooked your bacon, remove it from your skillet and saute the celery and onion in the bacon grease just long enough to add the dry ingredients as you get them ready. Still crunchy is good in potato salad. Stir in flour, sugar, salt, and pepper. Let it cook just long enough to give the mixture a tiny bit of a golden brown edge.

Add water and vinegar and stir until smooth. Pour your bacon and potatoes into the pan and stir to gently coat the potatoes and warm them. Serve this dish warm. Keep the leftovers! This potato salad is excellent served cold with your luncheon sandwiches at noon the next day as well as there is no mayonnaise in it to go sour.

Or, why wait until lunch? Mash the leftover ingredients, make potato cake patties and fry until golden brown on each side for breakfast.

SMOKIN' SAFETY

When I am going to put something in my grill and have hot briquettes doing the cooking, I will place my whole smoker either inside or right beside the camp site's fire pit. Safety is priority one! Always! It is always better to be safe than sorry.

~ Above: Canadian Geese and Goslings ~
Canada Geese mate for life. For this reason, when we were first married, I asked my husband (an avid hunter) to, please, not hunt them and he nicely agreed.

We are just visitors, it is their home,
help keep it G.R.E.E.N!

SMOKIN' GENERALITIES

Occasionally my husband and I will take along our little smoker on camping trips. It is lightweight and does not take up any more room than a cooler. I like having our smoker along on trips with our entire family. I can put the meat in to smoke in the morning and play the rest of the day until dinner time. I want to have fun camping too!

It is generally accepted that meat should smoke 45 minutes to an hour for each pound of meat at 250 degrees Fahrenheit. I admit, though, I usually just toss the meat in the smoker in the morning and forget it. But, before you "just forget it," it is wise to make sure your briquettes really are hot and smokin'! I have gone back to a cold smoker and raw meat because I got in a hurry and did not make sure my briquettes were burning.

If you are going to use wood chips, it is a good idea to soak them for fifteen minutes, or so, prior to placing in the smoker. Place your soaked wood chips or chunks in foil with holes poked in it or there is a small cast iron "box" available for just this purpose you can purchase. Choosing chips can be tough. Personally, my husband and I like hickory (of course), apple, cherry, pecan, and mesquite. Apple and pecan are really good with fish.

A Cottontail Rabbit munching some lunch. It is her home, help keep it G.R.E.E.N.

Barbecue Beef Brisket

5-6 pounds beef brisket or other meat,
    marinated in Red Meat Marinade
    (Get the center cut of the brisket!
        It is definitely worth the higher cost!)
2-3 large onions
1/2 cup chili sauce
1/2 cup barbecue sauce
1/2 cup Guiness beer or other beer of choice
Sprinkle with Tone's Roasted Garlic spice
Salt and pepper to taste
Add some smoke seasoning if you like

I prefer a dark beer with red meat and a light beer with white meat, but that is just my preference. Or if you do not like to use alcohol, 1/2 cup of beef stock or plain water will do. Or skip the salt and just add a bouillon cube to the water.

Start your coals in your barbecue grill, just like you were going to grill some burgers. You will not need the wire cooking grate for this. Place your Dutch oven on your coals in the grill bottom. With tongs, pull some briquettes around the side of the Dutch oven.

Pour the chili sauce, barbecue sauce, and liquid of choice into the Dutch oven. Mix until well combined. Place the brisket, with all of the marinade sauce into the mixture in the Dutch oven. Slice the onions and place them on top of the brisket. Add garlic cloves if you are a closet Italian like myself!

Put your lid on your Dutch oven and, again, using the tongs, place a few briquettes on top of the lid. Put the barbecue grill lid on top of your grill bottom with the Dutch oven inside. Open all barbecue grill vents to keep air circulating. You do not want to suffocate your briquettes. Let the brisket cook for 4-5 hours.

Dutch Oven Purist Wisdom

Okay, I know, there are a lot of Dutch oven purists out there right now moaning, "Nooo! Just surround your Dutch oven all over and around with coals and be done with it." I hear ya! There is just one problem with that. I do not want to sit around and watch my meat cook when I am camping. By putting my lid back on my grill with the Dutch oven inside and putting the whole thing in the camp site's fire pit, I feel more comfortable leaving my campsite to go play. Remember: Safety first, last, and always.

Smoked Yard Bird and Veggies

2 whole chickens
    smeared in vegetable oil and seasoning
Whole carrots and potatoes
    (Do not use baby vegetables.)
Wood chips specifically for smoking

Get your briquettes hot and smoking. Use enough briquettes to last for at least two or three hours. Put wood chips on top of briquettes.

Fill your water pan with water and add your carrots and potatoes. No need to cut these in pieces. Halve them at the very most. If they are cut any smaller, they will simply turn to mush. They are going to be smoked for at least a couple of hours so they do not need to be bite sized to cook.

Place your water pan and veggies in your smoker. Put your grill in place and place on it the two whole chickens with the breast side down. Cover your smoker with the lid and go play. When you return to your camp site that evening, your meal is totally ready. The chicken drippings will have seasoned the vegetables. Drain vegetables and serve.

On one particular camping trip one of our friends, Senior, told me that he did NOT like carrots - not in any way, shape, or form - thank you very much! After much cajoling and wheedling, we finally persuaded him to try the carrots I had cooked in the smoker water. Not only did he eat the one miniscule bite of carrot we all persuaded him to try, he had two large helpings before the meal was finished. His wife called me the next weekend laughing and telling me, "Guess what Senior cooked this weekend! Carrots in the smoker."

Herb Crusted Pork Tenderloin

If it is raining outside, this recipe cannot be beat for a toaster oven specialty! There is a little cleanup, but it is worth it all the way! The pesto paste and garlic paste can usually be found in the same area as the herb aisle in a tube or bottle. Or sometimes they can be found on display with the produce.

> 1 whole Pork Tenderloin (about three to four pounds)
> 1 cup Panko Bread Crumbs (Not regular bread crumbs)
> 1/2 ounce Italian Herb Mix
> 2 tablespoons vegetable oil
> 2 eggs
> 1 inch Amore Concentrated Pesto
> 1 inch Herb Shot Garlic Ajo
> 1 tablespoon Tone's Roasted Garlic
> 1 teaspoon Morton's Nature's Seasoning

Crack eggs into a bowl. Mix in the pesto and garlic paste. Add the Tone's Roasted Garlic and the Nature's Seasoning and stir.

In a separate bowl, mix the Panko bread crumbs and the Italian herbs. Regular bread crumbs are not recommended.

Dunk the tenderloin into the egg mixture and get it thoroughly wet. Next, put it in the herb and the bread crumb mixture and coat it all over thickly with the herbs and crumbs.

Heat oil in a skillet to a medium heat. Gently place the tenderloin in the skillet and very lightly brown it on all sides. Do not burn the bread crumbs or shake them loose.

Remove the tenderloin from the skillet and place it in a baking dish or on your toaster oven's baking tray. You may even put foil down first for easy cleanup.

Preheat toaster oven to 375 degrees Fahrenheit for at least ten minutes. Bake the tenderloin for 30 minutes until lightly pink or at least 155 degrees Fahrenheit in the middle.

Garden Fresh Grilled Sides

Asparagus	Pineapples Slices
Green beans	Plums
Egg plant	Pears
Yellow squash	Broccoli
Zucchini	Brussel sprouts

Veggie Preparation:

Bend asparagus until it snaps. Discard the bottom part, it is tough and woody. Snap ends off of green beans. Cut egg plant into 1/2 inch slices. Toss lightly in olive oil and place around the edges of the grill. Grill lightly. Veggies should still be slightly crisp when finished. Place in serving bowl and sprinkle with Vegetable Supreme veggie seasoning and serve.

Fruit Preparation:

Simply place pineapple on grill away from direct heat. Halve plums and remove seed. Halve pears and remove core. Place them cut side down on grill. The sugars in the fruit will carmalize, rendering these bites tasty as can be.

Crispy and Crumbly Dutch Oven Delight

If you are not using your Dutch oven for the main course, it works great for dessert also! Line your Dutch oven with aluminum foil. Pour two cans of any type of pie filling into the pan and spread evenly. In a separate bowl combine:

2 cups sugar
2 cups flour
1 cup oatmeal
1/2 cup chopped nuts
       (pecans or walnuts are great)
1 cup butter
1 teaspoon vanilla or other flavoring of choice
Cinnamon and/or nutmeg to taste

Mix these together until they are crumbly. Spread over the pie filling. Cover the Dutch oven and place on coals. I usually use 8-10 briquettes on the bottom and 14-15 on the top. Bake for 45-60 minutes until the top is golden brown and the fruit is bubbling.

Not in to making the "crisp" from scratch? Take a yellow cake mix, add oatmeal and nuts, and mix together. Sprinkle it over the top of the filling. Dot the mixture with chunks of butter. The cake mix works just as well as the scratch mix.

The Watermelon, Mint and Red Onion dish pictured was tried out of sheer curiosity. I thought, *"Mint, onion, and watermelon?!?!"* We liked it so well that I have since made it several times with a few of our own variations.

The original recipe called for mint leaves and basil leaves also - but, I am not a fan of that option. And, like most chefs on television, they said to spritz with lemon juice before serving. Not my thing. But, maybe you will try it that way.

Watermelon Wonder

1 small watermelon - seeded
1 small to medium sized sweet red onion
4 slices of bacon
1/2 cup sliced almonds, pecans, or walnuts
Salt and sugar or sweetener to taste

Cut your watermelon into bite-sized pieces, removing all of the seeds. (This is time consuming, but this salad is worth it!) Put the chunks into a big bowl. Add the nuts. Fry the bacon, pat all of the grease off of it, and crumble into the watermelon. Chop the onion into small pieces and stir into the bowl. Add salt and sugar to taste.

Warrant Officer Watermelon Surprise

1 small watermelon - seeded
4 large to huge tomatoes (try yellow ones for color)
2 pounds sweet Bing cherries (optional)
1 quart ripe strawberries (optional)
1 pkg instant Black Cherry (or other) flavored gelatin
Salt and fresh ground pepper to taste
3 cups boiling water and 3 cups cold water

Bring the water to a full boil. Blanch the tomatoes just a minute or two. Remove them and submerge them in the cold water. Peel tomatoes. Remove seeds from everything, even the tomatoes, and cut into bite-sized pieces in a large bowl. Pour all of the fruit and tomato juice into a separate bowl. Mix in the instant gelatin until dissolved. Pour the mixture back over salad and stir thoroughly. Salt and pepper (yes, the pepper is key!) to taste. Chill overnight and serve.

Chief Warrant Officer Watermelon Wow

1 small watermelon	3 medium cucumbers
1 large red onion	1/3 cup raspberry vinegar
1/8 cup olive oil	1/4 cup sugar
Celery salt & pepper to taste	1 pkg Raspberries

Seed and cut watermelon and cucumbers into bite sized pieces. Mix all ingredients in a bowl, refrigerate and marinate. Garnish with raspberries. (Frozen will work just fine.)

Watermelon Salad Variations
Instead of using gelatin, use a flavored yogurt.
Add brown sugar instead of white sugar.
Sprinkle with cinnamon or nutmeg.
Use a flavored vodka for an adult twist.
If using almonds, use some Amaretto liqueur as well.
Use all melon: Watermelon, Cantaloupe, Mush Melon.
Use the watermelon rind as the bowl.
Toss with shredded coconut instead of chives.
Toss in some Mandarin Oranges or Blood Oranges.
Use sweet red beats as a variation to tomatoes.
To add some crunch, chop up some celery in the salad.
Serve over iceberg lettuce for a different crunch.
Serve over spinach or add fresh chopped spinach
        instead of the basil or mint suggested earlier.
A chives or mint garnish may add the finishing touch.

Watermelon Vodka Woo Hoo
Blend or puree either the Watermelon Surprise or the Watermelon Wow with ice. Add vodka and enjoy.

Mellody's Bloody Best
Bloody Mary in the World

Chill your glasses ahead of time by placing them in the cooler. Run a lime around the lip of the glass. Roll glass rim in Bloody Mary Salt. Fill the glass with ice. Squeeze the rest of the juice onto the ice. Now you are ready to add the good stuff!

Mellody's Simple Mary

1 shot of a good vodka (Grey Goose)
3 ounces V-8
3 ounces Zing Zang Bloody Mary Mix

Pour 1.5 oz vodka over ice, add V-8, Zing Zang, and stir or shake. (I prefer to shake my Bloody Mary's just a tad. Do not shake until the tomato juice is frothy. Shake just enough to mix all of the ingredients well.)

Mellody's Favorite Merry Mary:

Worcestershire Sauce - 1/8 tsp
Chipotle Tabasco Sauce - 3 drops
Twang Bloody Mary Salt (around rim)
Seasoned pepper and celery salt - sprinkled on ice
Green Olive juice - 1 tablespoon
Sweet Merlot Wine - 2 tablespoons
Dill pickle *or* sauerkraut juice - 1 teaspoon
A drop of Liquid Smoke
> Garnish with a dill pickle spear, green olives, a celery stalk, and a lime wedge.

I Think I Am Part Italian Bloody Mary
Cherry Wine - 2 tablespoons
Spice World Smoked Garlic smashed to a pulp
      (plus a little of the juice - 3 or 4 drops)
Celery Salt and Morton's Nature's Seasoning to taste
Pepperoncini juice - 1 tablespoon
Garnish with a celery stalk and pepperoncinis

I Love Oriental Food Bloody Mary
Plum Wine - 2 tablespoons   Wasabi Paste - 1/8 inch or so
Woeber's Smoky Horseradish - 1/8 inch or so, flavored to taste
Chili powder to taste   Garnish with cocktail onions

Bloody Mary Variations
Use flavored lemon citrus vodka or bacon-infused vodka. Use bourbon or Spicy V-8. (Especially good when used in the Oriental Mary.) Use Beef bouillon instead of V-8 (or use both). Add a touch of Dijon mustard for a flavor kick.

Bloody Mary Salt
If you cannot find it pre-packaged, mix the following together: One part lemon-lime salt, one part dill salt, and one part chili mix. Another option: Mix table salt and cayenne pepper.

Mellody's BLT is NOT a Sandwich!
1 shot bacon-infused bourbon (Wild Turkey)   3 ounces V-8
1 teaspoon maple syrup   3 ounces Zing Zang Mix
Hickory salt to taste. Pour over ice, shake just once, and enjoy!

To infuse alcohol with bacon: Fry four strips of very good smoked bacon. Pour the cooled, but not solidified, fat into a quart jar with a good bourbon or vodka. Let sit at room temperature eight hours to three weeks. Yes, weeks. Put jar in freezer overnight. The next morning, remove the congealed fat with a spoon and strain the alcohol back into its bottle.

Favorite Camping Recipes

_____

_____

_____

_____

_____

_____

_____

_____

_____

_____

_____

_____

_____

_____

_____

_____

Favorite Camping Recipes

_____

_____

_____

_____

_____

_____

_____

_____

_____

_____

_____

_____

_____

_____

_____

_____

_____

Favorite Camping Recipes

Favorite Camping Recipes

_____

_____

_____

_____

_____

_____

_____

_____

_____

_____

_____

_____

_____

_____

_____

Favorite Camping Recipes

Favorite Camping Recipes

_____

_____

_____

_____

_____

_____

_____

_____

_____

_____

_____

_____

_____

_____

_____

_____

Favorite Camping Recipes

_____

_____

_____

_____

_____

_____

_____

_____

_____

_____

_____

_____

_____

_____

_____

_____

_____

Above: Our 2002 is still looking brand new.
Below: Checking the safety straps and bar
bolts holding our bicycles on the rack.

Chapter Six
~ Sorbet ~
Cleaning Your Palette

Equipment Maintenance and Care

I think most of us could probably perform more maintenance on our vehicles we drive every day. We could certainly take better care of them. I see worn tires, broken lights, and cracked windshields almost every day when driving around. I am sure you do too. Oddly enough, we seem take better care of our pop-ups and campers, it seems. Maybe it is because we do not use them as much. Maybe it is because we keep them longer and need them to last better.

I remember the time my husband and I went to trade in one of our used pop-ups for our brand new Coleman and we told the dealer, "Our pop-up is like new." Of course the dealer gave us this really skeptical look.

I looked at him at said, "I mean it. It's not a used pop-up in good condition. It's a used pop-up in 'like new' condition. I'm not exaggerating!" Still skeptical, he said, "Okay, bring it in. I'll take a look at it."

The next weekend we pulled our pop-up onto his lot and let him look. He did not hesitate and he did not quibble over the amount we wanted in trade-in. He snapped it up. Our pop-ups are resale clean! The following tips will hopefully help you keep your pop-up resale clean also.

As I said in the beginning, I am not a mechanic and I am not an engineer. My tips are geared toward general care and upkeep - not mechanical repair or replacement. Most of that information is in your Owner's Manual.

Fire Extinguisher

Keep a fire extinguisher in your camper at all times. Most campers actually have a designated storage spot for this item. You need to know, however, that fire extinguishers are rated into three major types.

Class A: Wood, paper, cloth, rubber, and some plastics.

Class B: Flammable liquids, such as grease, motor oil, paint thinner, and gasoline.

Class C: Electrical equipment.

Be sure that you have the correct fire extinguisher in your camper for your situation. Also, fire extinguishers need to be inspected regularly. Most fire departments are happy to do this for you.

Note: Do NOT check your extinguisher yourself by spraying it, even for a moment. Once sprayed, it will gradually lose pressure and will not be fully charged for use in an emergency.

Be sure to read all the paperwork accompanying your fire extinguisher and to keep it in a safe place.

My husband and stepson readying the air conditioning unit for installment.

Condensation

Condensation is a pop-up camper's enemy. While cooking inside, open the roof vent and/or crack the vinyl window closest to the stove. If you have your window cracked, this means you will have your canvas window cover rolled down. Place a hand towel over the rolled canvas to keep grease from splattering the canvas.

If you have a shower and use it, turn the air conditioner on or open the windows for air circulation when done. Proper ventilation will prevent excessive condensation. You want your camper dry when stored. The consequences of mold and mildew could be nasty.

Stove and Sink

Whenever you go camper shopping, one of the first things to look at is the cook stove. If it has a lot of rust or chips on the stove, move on to the next possibility. It has never ceased to amaze me over the years the number of stoves I have seen that have had cooked-on food literally welded to them. It is easy to keep your stove clean if you wipe the messes up immediately.

Once a stove is stored in a camper with the top down, that food will gradually eat away at the enamel and will leave actual "pitted" spots in the enamel. Do not store your pop-up until your stove is clean and dry.

That goes for your sink as well. Remember to make sure you have turned off your faucet prior to turning on the main water spigot. Turn your faucet on slowly to bleed the air.

The Refrigerator

I am royally, overboard, persnickety about some things. I admit it. And, one of those things is mold and mildew. I use my portable refrigerator with its teeny-tiny freezer every camping trip and there is absolutely no way to get it perfectly dry prior to putting the top down. However, I have never opened my camper to a moldy, mildewy mess either. My trick? It is actually something I learned from my Mom.

When you are getting ready to tear down your campsite, the first thing to do is to empty the refrigerator and freezer and put all the food back into the coolers. Turn the refrigerator off. Take two or three towels and put them inside the refrigerators and freezer. Leave the doors open with the towels inside and start packing away other items.

Your towels will soon be soaked from the condensation that drips off of the inside walls of the unit as it "warms up" to

The paper absorbs any moisture and the cedar blocks absorb any odor. If you are wondering, yes, you can usually use the same newspaper over and over again for at least one whole camping season.
(I know it looks a bit strange, but it works!
And, I have never had mildew or mold.)

the outside temperature. You may have to change towels and put dry ones in for a second absorption round. Once the inside of the unit has "warmed up" and the condensation has ceased, completely dry out the unit with more fresh towels.

Place plenty of lightly wadded up newspaper inside the unit. I keep the same newspaper to use over and over. While camping, I just take the newspaper out and store it in a trashbag out of the way until it is needed at the end of our trip.

I also place several blocks of cedar inside the refrigerator when storing it. The paper and the cedar blocks absorb any dampness that I may have overlooked and I never worry about mildew. You can find the cedar blocks in almost any department store in the households aisle.

My stepson and husband working on his pop-up. Here they are preparing the wiring to install the AC. Canvas solar covers will greatly increase the efficiency of the air conditioning unit.

As an extra precaution, my husband and I never store our refrigerators with the doors totally closed either. We always leave them open just a smidgen to allow the air to circulate. We have never opened our refrigerators and had mold or mildew after storing them by using this method.

Lighting the Refrigerator and Water Heater

When setting up camp, if you have a propane heated refrigerator and/or water heater, it will be much easier to light them if you first light your stove on the inside. By lighting your stove first, you will purge the air out of the propane line while lighting something easily accessed.

EXTREMELY IMPORTANT SAFETY NOTE:

Sometimes a gust of wind might extinguish your water heater pilot. Should this happen, turn your propane gas OFF and wait at least five minutes to re-light. The waiting period allows any unburned gas to dissipate.

RE-LIGHT TOO SOON ~ MAKE A BIG BOOM!

Carpeting

The first thing my husband and I do when we get a new-used pop-up is put in carpeting. Yes, carpeting. It saves the linoleum from all the gravel dents and dirt scratches. When we go to trade the pop-up, we pull the carpet up and have brand new-looking linoleum.

We have been able to carpet our pop-up camper for less than $25.00 each and every time. We usually can purchase a carpet remnant from a carpet dealer. My sister-in-law used two area rugs from a department store and used carpet tape to hold them together and hide the joined cut.

Both my sister-in-law and I keep a small hand vac in our pop-ups and vacuum right before closing the camper down. It takes maybe ten minutes from start to finish and it is the last thing to do before lowering the top.

Laying carpet may not be the logical thing to do, however, if you have children. I would imagine that children would track in more mud than just my husband and I do. It is a toss up. A carpet to keep vacuumed or linoleum to sweep and mop? It depends on your situation.

"Tenting" and Vinyl Canvas

Keeping the vinyl "tenting" or canvas clean is probably one of the biggest challenges. When lowering your camper and you get to the half-way point, pull your canvas out over the ends of the bunk and let it hang. Take a broom and sweep off the dust and leaves and such before folding the canvas back onto the beds for storage.

The only time to really wash your canvas properly is when it is popped up. My husband and I do this religiously once a year. After we have camped for the last time in the fall.

Cleaning the canvas is not easy. First of all you do not want to use any harsh chemicals on it that will degrade the vinyl canvas and its water-proof characteristics. Read your Owner's Manual for the recommended product specific to your pop-up tenting. Although I have not tried it, a product called InstaGone has received good reviews.

Second of all, it is cloth - so to speak. There is nothing to lean on while you are angling toward the center to get it clean! It is a stretch even for a tall person.

Your best bet is a ladder, a bucket of warm water, whichever type of detergent or cleaner is recommended in the camper's Owner's Manual, a very soft cloth on a long handle, and a water hose. Rinse the dust off with a quick dousing of water. Be careful when rinsing and avoid spraying water into your furnace or refrigerator vents. Dip your soft cloth into a bucket of recommended cleaner and water and very gently scrub the canvas. Do not bear down. Do not use a scratch pad.

As a general rule, use automotive vinyl cleaner and not detergent. Detergents and other solvents will cause damage to the vinyl. After you have scrubbed your canvas/vinyl clean, rinse it well. Keep your camper popped up until the canvas is thoroughly dry and then put it back down. While it is down, unzip your awning and clean it in the same manner, letting it fully dry before storing.

Tires and Wheels

Always check your tire pressure before taking off on a trip. And do not forget to check the spare! While you are at it, check the lug nuts. They can work themselves loose.

Do the "penny" check. Turn a penny upside down and place between the tire treads. Measure the lowest point in the tread. If you can see above Lincoln's head or any part of the letters, "In God We Trust," you need a new tire. Check the tires at several locations.

When you pull into a station for a rest stop, reach down and feel your wheel hubs. If they are extremely hot you may have a wheel bearing going bad. Or maybe they just need to be repacked. This is recommended every 5,000 miles or so as is a tire rotation.

Canvas Solar Covers

This summer, for the first time, my stepson purchased solar bunkend covers. He loves them! He says he can tell they make a significant difference in the temperature inside the camper and the AC does not have to work as hard to keep the camper cool. I have read good reviews on them and cannot wait to try them. Not only will they help keep my canvas clean when set up, they are heat reflective. On hot summer days, they will help keep heat out. On cool autumn nights, they will help to keep heat in. I am looking forward to using these.

Sides and Roof Top

Check your Owner's Manual for the recommended cleaning product. These can be a challenge to clean. They get this black stuff on them that is a combination of tree sap, dirt, and road oil. After a summer of camping it seems to weld to the camper sidewalls and the roof top like cement glue.

There are several products advertised to take this stuff off and I have yet to find one that works as well as it is advertised. Especially on the top of the camper.

It seems to just take a good amount of old-fashioned elbow grease. Once you do have it clean, though, apply a coat of Turtle Wax Car Paste. Again, this is not the quickest or easiest product on the market to work with - but, it does do the job! Follow the directions on the can.

It is best to work in the shade, also. You do not want to have to try to rub this stuff off after it has baked on. Trust me on this one. And, yes, I am once again, unfortunately, speaking from experience. Where was my husband when I made this particular goof?

Apply the coat of Turtle Wax and buff it off good. This will make cleaning your camper's sides and roof a lot easier the next time you tackle the job.

Many of the handles on a camper, inside and out, are plastic or inexpensive molded metal. Be gentle with them. Also, the plastic water spouts on the outside of the camper need a gentle touch.

Do <u>NOT</u> Force It!

Whether you are putting your pop-up up or pulling it down, you should never have to force anything! Read this sentence again. Do NOT force it!

If something is stuck, then something is not right. Do not force it. Figure out what is wrong and make the correction. For instance, if your door drags, chances are your camper is not sufficiently level.

Do not raise your camper top so far that the guide wire is screaming tight. That is way too much. It should just be barely taut, with a slight wiggle left in it.

If this guide wire (ours is red) is not on the camper that you are considering purchasing, find out why.

Does that model have a different method to prevent over-cranking or was the roof over-cranked and it broke?

The "Do NOT Force It!" rule is especially applicable to the drawers and cabinet doors in a pop-up. Do not let them just "snap" in place when closing them. Press the handle down, as you would when opening them. Those handles are not very sturdy on the best of campers. If you do not want to replace them, just depress the button both when opening and closing them. Because these handles are so fragile, we keep a couple of extra in our camper.

NOTES:

Tools Kept Inside the Camper

_____ Small level

_____ Wheel chocks

_____ Leveling boards

_____ Rope

_____ Crank and/or Socket Jenie

_____ Tire jack

_____ Clean water hose

_____ Dumping hose

_____ Electrical cords, heavy-duty and light-duty

Variable Tools:

_____

_____

_____

_____

_____

_____

Tool Box Check List

Always keep the Army's favorite assets on hand:
A roll of duct tape and WD-40. Because, "If it moves and it isn't supposed to, use the duct tape. If it doesn't move and it is supposed to, use WD-40."

_____ Small axe/hatchet and/or camp saw

_____ Hammer (large enough to drive stakes)

_____ Small shovel (see Army surplus types)

_____ Screwdrivers - the most commonly used:
        Flathead, Phillips, Robertson, & Hex

_____ Adjustable wrench or a wrench set

_____ Pliers and needle-nosed pliers

_____ Ratchet and socket set

_____ Pocket knife and/or multi tool (in a pinch)

_____ Cable ties and assorted bungee straps

_____ Jumper cables

_____ Flashlight

_____ Tire pressure gauge

_____ Drill - 24 volt if using Socket Jenie

_____ DC/AC Adapter

Winterizing Your Pop-Up Camper

_____ Read your owner's manual and follow the specific instructions for your make and model of pop-up. If you do not have an owner's manual, most can be requested online.

_____ Do a "fall" cleaning. Vacuum everything: the carpet, the seats, the mattresses, and the curtains.

_____ Wipe the wood down with a good furniture polish. Wood does need this care.

_____ Clean and dry the stove, the sink, and the refrigerator. Prepare refrigerator for storage as previously instructed to prevent mold and mildew.

_____ Clean the plastic "windows" with a soft cloth and window cleaner or a vinegar and water solution. Dry.

_____ Remove anything from your camper that could freeze and burst. This includes all canned goods, jars, lotions, soaps, and liquids, plus the flashlight batteries.

_____ Insure every electrical appliance and all switches are turned off.

_____ Place cedar blocks and, if you wish, dryer sheets inside cupboards, all drawers, in all nooks and crannies, in the corners on the floor, and on top of beds and furniture.
 Cedar blocks are my favorite and serve three purposes:
   a. They help absorb moisture.
   b. They are a bug and spider deterrent.
   c. They absorb odors and smell great.

_____ Cover your AC unit.

_____ Remove the battery. It will simply discharge in 30 to 45 days and could freeze in cold weather.

_____ Double-check and make sure the propane is off and cover the propane tank or tanks, if more than one.

_____ If you have a power jack, cover it.

_____ Chock wheels and cover tires. If you do not have a dry place to park your pop-up, roll it up onto boards prior to parking it for the winter.

_____ If not under a cover, such as a car port, then tilt the camper slightly to encourage meltoff and runoff.

_____ Empty water tank, water heater, and drain all lines, both incoming and outgoing. This includes cassette toilet and shower. Do not forget outside shower lines, if so equipped.

_____ Clean the grey and black water tanks.

_____ If you live in a part of the country that has freezing weather over the winter, once everything is drained, put RV antifreeze* back into your lines and run the lines until you see the antifreeze.

_____ Close and cover all valves and openings on the outside of the trailer. Critters will find them and/or wasps will build nests in them.

*NOTE: Use ONLY an RV antifreeze. Do NOT use automotive antifreeze. RV antifreeze is not toxic. Rinse and flush thoroughly and completely when getting ready to go on your first trip in the Spring.

Getting Ready for the First Trip of the Year

_____ Remove all covers from valves and openings.

_____ Check your battery charge and hook up. Ensure your battery is secured correctly.

_____ Remove AC cover and check it over. Clean filter.

_____ Check inside screws holding AC unit to ceiling. Turn it on and make sure it is running good.

_____ Remove tire covers and check pressure.

_____ Check tires for any bumps, tread separations, or any other noticeable defect.

_____ Check the spare tire.

_____ Check all exterior lights.

_____ Check and lubricate the stabilizers, locks, and hinges.

_____ Uncover, check, and hook up propane tank.

_____ Light stove and insure it is in good working condition.

_____ Light your refrigerator. Switch to electric. Make sure both systems are working correctly.

_____ Hook up to running water. Flush out the anti-freeze. Run all taps until crystal clear water appears, then turn off.

_____ Fill freshwater tank with water. Check for any leaks. If no noticeable leaks, add bleach or pool chlorine to the tank.

_____ Use about 1/2 cup of bleach to a 30 gallon water tank.

_____ Turn faucets on and let water run until you smell the bleach/chlorine. Turn off. Let water set in tank and lines for at least three hours.

_____ Empty tank. Fill with fresh water and drain.

_____ Fill water tank again with fresh water. Drain again.

_____ It is best not to travel with a full tank of water. Do not fill again until you reach the campgrounds.

_____ Hook up your tow vehicle and test all of the electrical connections.

The cats object to being left behind and will often sit in or on top of our suitcases to show their displeasure.

So, every once in a while we take them with us. Yes, cats can enjoy camping, too. Just don't forget the litter box!

PUBs
(Pop-Up Blunders - Not the local "watering" hole.)

_____ Remember to raise your stabilizers and jack before heading out. And lock your hitch!

_____ Close your ceiling vent before lowering the roof. You know why.

_____ If you cannot find your keys, look on top of the camper, especially if it is already raised.

_____ Do not throw dead batteries into the campfire. They will explode and the flying shrapnel is dangerous!

_____ Close and lock the door securely, otherwise you may be traveling down the road only to look in your side mirror and see it flapping in the wind.

_____ Fold up and secure the towel rack/clothes hanger rod that hangs from the ceiling <u>prior</u> to lowering the roof.

_____ Do not leave your crank handle in the roof jack. Someone down the road will find it, but you will not know who and you will be out one crank handle.

BEST ADVICE:

READ YOUR OWNER'S MANUAL.

**No statement made in this book
is meant to counter anything
in your Owner's Manual.**

Your Own Best PUBs - Come on, Fess up:

_____

_____

_____

_____

_____

_____

_____

_____

_____

_____

_____

_____

_____

My Favorite Websites:

mdc.mo.gov

mostreamteam.org

popuptimes.com

popupexplorer.com

rvupgradestore.com

reserveamerica.com

rvworkshop.com

tossinggames.com

recipelink.com

*Disclaimer: Neither the author nor the publisher are responsible for the accuracy, content, or correctness of any web site references used in this publication. Nor is the author or publisher responsible for computer viruses or any other computer interruption users may encounter searching the web. These websites are referenced only as a point of interest and an additional source of entertaining information. If you do not want to be bound by the preceding disclaimer, do not research these or any other referred to links.

"I like to think I can sometimes - just for a brief second - feel God's heavenly *Paradise* in whispers of moments spent in nature. And when I am camping, I let that feeling seep deep into my soul. I hope you will too."

An interesting bark
formation on a tree.

Packed and all ready to go again.

Phyllis Rossiter said in her book, *A Living History of the Ozarks*, "Here in the Ozarks you *feel* the country, experience it, rather than just admire it. For those who seek it, a sweet serenity dwells here, a restful tranquility."

She is so right and I hope no matter where your travels take you; that you are rewarded with that same miracle of nature's tranquility on your next camping trip.

I would also like to thank again, from the bottom of my heart, the professionals who read my book and gave it good reviews. My book turned out so much better due to your suggestions and helpful remarks. Thank you. Thank you! Thank you!

Mellody R.L. Allee

RECIPES

Some of my favorite books:

Missouri Wildflowers
by Edgar Denison
Published by the Missouri Department of
Conservation

The Complete Katy Trail Guidebook
by Brett Dufur
Published by Pebble Publishing and reprinted
courtesy of the Missouri Department of Natural
Resources

Wild Edibles of Missouri
by Jan Phillips
Published by the Missouri Department of
Conservation

A Living History of the Ozarks
by Phyllis Rossiter
Published by Pelican Publishing Company, Inc.

Birds of Missouri Field Guide
by Stan Tekiela
Published by Adventure Publications, Inc.

*The Audubon Society Field Guide to North
American Mushrooms*
by Gary H. Lincoff
Published by Alfred A. Knopf, Inc.

When she was still in high school, Mellody checked "join the military" on her ACT. With her father's encouragement, she joined the Army at 17 and went on to spend 25 years serving her country. Before she retired, Mellody returned to college to study literature. She wanted to learn what made a book endure through the ages to become a classic. While she may never write a classic, she is grateful her military career paid for her education and inspired her first book, *Camping in a Pop-Up Camper is Paradise.*

When Mellody is not writing or camping, she can be found walking, biking, or running the Champ-meister, taking pictures of nature, cooking, reading, painting, or playing pool. She lives in the Show Me state's Ozarks with her husband, three cats, a pygmy goat, a miniature horse, a miniature Missouri mule, and any wild critters she can attract to her yard.

CPSIA information can be obtained at www.ICGtesting.com
Printed in the USA
LVOW01s1139201213

365892LV00008B/305/P